Cybersecurity in the COVID-19 Pandemic

Cybersecurity in the COVID-19 Pandemic

Kenneth Okereafor

CRC Press
Taylor & Francis Group
Boca Raton London New York

CRC Press is an imprint of the
Taylor & Francis Group, an **informa** business

First edition published 2021
by CRC Press
6000 Broken Sound Parkway NW, Suite 300, Boca Raton, FL 33487-2742

and by CRC Press
2 Park Square, Milton Park, Abingdon, Oxon, OX14 4RN

© 2021 Taylor & Francis Group, LLC

CRC Press is an imprint of Taylor & Francis Group, an Informa business

No claim to original U.S. Government works

ISBN-13: 978-0-367-61091-3 (hbk)
ISBN-13: 978-0-367-72143-5 (pbk)

Typeset in Computer Modern font
by KnowledgeWorks Global Ltd.

This book is dedicated in sympathy to all victims of cybercrime during the COVID-19 pandemic, in condolence to all bereaved families during the same period, and in goodwill to a global audience that is desirous of Cybersecurity knowledge.

Contents

Preface

The motivation for this book began shortly after completing my PhD research at the UNESCO International Centre for Theoretical Physics (ICTP) in Italy in 2017 when my longing to share technology knowledge and cause positive change transformed into a passion, upon realizing that many people only view Cybersecurity as a mirage, an enigma, something to be dreaded. I had longed for the opportunity to demystify many of the Cybersecurity concepts, and I wanted real-world scenarios that people can comfortably relate with.

The opportunity finally came amid the mandatory lockdown that forced everyone to work from home as a precautionary measure to control the spread of the novel coronavirus disease that was later codenamed COVID-19 by the World Health Organization (WHO) on the 11th of February 2020. At that point I knew the time was ripe to put pen to paper and capture the bubbling cyberspace activities, most of which manifested as various levels of vulnerabilities and exposures to cyberattacks.

Following numerous feedback I received after my first COVID-19 publication in February 2020 titled: *"Tackling the Cybersecurity Impacts of the Coronavirus Outbreak as a Challenge to Internet Safety",* I was convinced that the stage was set to pursue my passion and fulfil a destiny.

Today, the rest is history as I present *Cybersecurity in the COVID-19 Pandemic* as a legacy to everyone who relies on online services and digital assets for communications, interactions, information exchange, leisure, business, education, and worship.

I hope the book helps the reader to earn a better understanding of how best to prevent, detect, and respond to cyber attacks as we interact with digital resources in our daily personal and corporate lives, particularly in the post COVID-19 digital era.

Kenneth Okereafor

Foreword

Kenneth Okereafor is a Nigerian whose intellect and drive inspire hope that a better tomorrow is possible for all of us, especially for the upcoming generation. Kenneth's lucid writing style eases the reader into a variety of important issues that encompass Cybersecurity and COVID-19 Pandemic.

Cybersecurity in the COVID-19 Pandemic is an excellent contribution from a serious Cybersecurity researcher, biometric expert, and cyberspace defender. Each part of the eight-chapter book introduces and outlines important Cybersecurity concepts using real-world illustrations from the pandemic to make the narrative engaging, educative, and impactful. Kenneth succinctly outlines the online breaches and Cybersecurity incidents observed during the pandemic and highlights the relevant Cybersecurity lessons.

Cybersecurity in the COVID-19 Pandemic is a useful Cybersecurity companion that should be in the library of strategic decision makers, technical, operational and administrative managers, students of technology, seekers of knowledge, and those who are responsible for managing, or those significantly impacted by, technology risk.

I recommend *Cybersecurity in the COVID-19 Pandemic*.

Abdul-Hakeem Ajijola,
Chair, Consultancy Support Services Ltd,
NIGERIA.
info@consultancyss.com

Acknowledgements

My utmost gratitude goes to God Almighty for igniting my passion, providing my strength, and sustaining my health throughout the rigours of the book project, from start to finish. I sincerely appreciate my family members for their patience, understanding and emotional encouragement; and I am grateful to friends and professional colleagues for their intellectual support.

Special thanks to Ms. Gabriella Williams, Editor, and Mr. Daniel Kershaw, Editorial Assistant at CRC Press who arranged the initial manuscripts, prepared drafts, and coordinated the reviews and administrative support.

I wish to acknowledge and appreciate the kind contributions and support of the following individuals and organizations towards the success of this book.

- Prof. Oliver Osuagwu, Professor of Computer Science, Imo State University, Nigeria.
- Mr. Abdul-Hakeem Ajijola, Chair, African Union Cyber Security Expert Group, Chair Consultancy Support Services Ltd, Nigeria.
- Prof. Raymond Akwule, Emeritus Faculty, George Mason University, Washington DC, US.
- Prof. Anil Jain, Professor of Computer Science, Michigan State University, US.
- Prof. Alvin B. Marcelo, Professor of Surgery and Health Informatics, University of the Philippines, Manila.
- Prof. Mohammed N. Sambo, Professor of Health Policy and Management, Executive Secretary, National Health Insurance Scheme (NHIS), Nigeria.
- Mr. Nasiru Ikharo, General Manager, Department of Information and Communications Technology, National Health Insurance Scheme (NHIS), Nigeria.
- Dr. Jonathan Eke, General Manager, Formal Sector Department, National Health Insurance Scheme (NHIS), Nigeria.
- Uche M. Mbanaso, PhD, Executive Director, Centre for Cyberspace Studies, Nasarawa State University, Keffi, Nigeria.
- Mr. Adelaiye Oluwasegun, Department of Computer Science, Bingham University Karu, Nigeria.
- O. Paul Isikaku-Ironkwe, Director, B. T. Matthias Labs, RTSD Technologies, San Diego, California 92101, US.

- Mr. Chike Onwuegbuchi, Deputy Editor-in-chief, Nigeria Communications Week.
- Dr. Olajide Joseph Adebola, Chief Technology Officer/Partner, Home Plus Medicare Services Ltd. Abuja, Nigeria.
- Mr. Phil Manny, Director West Africa – Alliance Media Group, Founder & Director, Agora Nexus.
- Engr. Rania Djehaiche, Mohamed El Bachir El Ibrahimi University of Bordj Bou Arreridj, Algeria.

For all individuals and organizations whose constructive critiques helped to improve the quality of this book, I thank you most sincerely.

About the Author

 **Kenneth Okereafor** holds a PhD in Cybersecurity & Biometrics from Azteca University Mexico, and an MSc in Computer Security and BSc in Computer Information Systems from American Heritage University of Southern California, US. As a Deputy General Manager at Nigeria's National Health Insurance Scheme (NHIS), he currently coordinates database security and health informatics, develops and facilitates Cybersecurity education curriculum, and leads the enterprise software security team.

A United Nations–trained expert in threat mitigation technologies with over 25 years global experience in Cybersecurity & Biometrics across industry, government, and academia, Kenneth has developed and implemented Cybersecurity processes and curricula for preventing cybercrimes, detecting cyber threats, and responding to cyber breaches within the Nigerian health insurance ecosystem, resulting in superlative improvements in the safe management of sensitive healthcare data and digital identities among stakeholders.

As a Cybersecurity expert, he participated in the three-year development of Nigeria's first eHealth Strategy which was completed and adopted for operationalization in 2016, and he has since remained actively involved in its implementation, particularly in developing sound Cybersecurity protocols for stakeholders involved in the generation, use, and exchange of sensitive healthcare data.

A former employee of the US Department of State, and an alumnus scientist of the UNESCO International Centre for Theoretical Physics (ICTP) in Italy, Kenneth chairs the Technical Committee & National Mirror Committee (TC & NMC) of the International Organization for Standardization ISO-TC/215 Health Informatics Working Group 4 – *Security and Privacy*, in Nigeria, developing Cybersecurity standards for Nigeria's eHealth sector.

Kenneth possesses a second PhD in the Administration & Management of Information and Communications Technology (ICT) from Central University of Nicaragua, and has published several peer reviewed papers on Cybersecurity and Socio-technical impacts, Data Protection, Biometric Liveness Detection, Digital Forensics, Electronic Health, and Telemedicine.

List of Tables

List of Figures

List of Acronyms

2FA	Two-Factor Authentication
9/11	September 11, 2001 terrorist attack
AI	Artificial Intelligence
AIC	Availability, Integrity, and Confidentiality
ATM	Automated Teller Machine
BAS	Biometric Authentication System
BD	Big Data
BEC	Business Email Compromise
BSSN	Badan Siber dan Sandi Negara (Indonesia's National Cyber and Encryption Agency)
BTC	Bit coin
CANSO	Civil Air Navigation Services Organization
CCTV	Closed Circuit Television
CDC	Centers for Disease Control
CEO	Chief Executive Officer
CERRT	Computer Emergency Readiness and Response Team
CIA	Central Intelligence Agency
CIA	Confidentiality, Integrity, and Availability
CIR	Computer Incident Response
CoV	Coronavirus family
COVID-19	Coronavirus disease
DDoS	Distributed Denial of Service
DHHS	Department of Health and Human Services
DiD	Digital Identity
DoS	Department of State, also Denial of Service
EFCC	Economic and Financial Crimes Commission
EHR	Electronic Health Record
eID	Electronic Identity
EoI	Events of Interest
FBI	Federal Bureau of Investigation
GCA	Global Cybersecurity Agenda
GPS	Global Positioning Satellite
HIE	Health Information Exchange
HIPAA	Health Insurance Portability and Accountability Act
ICCAIA	International Coordinating Council of Aerospace Industries Associations

ICT	Information and Communications Technology
IDS	Intrusion Detection System
IEEE	Institute of Electrical and Electronic Engineers
IETF	Internet Engineering Task Force
IoC	Indicators of Compromise
IoT	Internet of Things
IPS	Intrusion Prevention System
ITU	International Telecommunication Union
MERS	Middle East Respiratory Syndrome
NBT	Next Big Thing
NCC	Nigerian Communications Commission
NHC	(Chinese) National Health Commission
NHIS	National Health Insurance Scheme
NIST	National Institute of Standards and Technology
NITDA	National Information Technology Development Agency
NNID	Nintendo Network ID
NSA	National Security Agency
NSW	New South Wales
OS	Operating System
PHEIC	Public Health Emergency of International Concern
PHI	Protected Health Information
PHR	Personal Health Record
PII	Personally Identifiable Information
PKI	Public Key Infrastructure
PPE	Personal Protective Equipment
SANS	System Administration, Networking and Security
SCADA	Supervisory Control and Data Acquisition
SEC	Securities and Exchange Commission
SFO	San Francisco International Airport
SMB	Server Message Block
SMS	Short Message Service
SQL	Structured Query Language
SSL	Secure Sockets Layer
SSO	Single Sign-on
TLS	Transport Layer Security
UK	United Kingdom
URL	Uniform Resource Locator
US	United States
VOIP	Voice over Internet Protocol
WFH	Work from Home
WHO	World Health Organization

Introduction: COVID-19 Pandemic, the Game Changer

1

1.1 COVID-19 PANDEMIC, THE GAME CHANGER

There were no year 2020 predictions that came close to the magnitude of devastation caused by the outbreak of the coronavirus disease.

It is unbelievable how global events turned out so dramatically in 2020, particularly how the cyberspace became disrupted, not by a devastating atomic bomb or a trans-ocean teletsunami but by a mere biological virus whose infinitesimal diameter is estimated to be only approximately 125 nanometers, or equivalent to 600 times smaller than the diameter of the human hair; that is the novel coronavirus, pathogen that ignited the pandemic, the game changer.

2020 plans and budgets were disrupted [1], everyday life was impacted [2], and the world came to a standstill as authorities compelled people to stay at and work from home (WFH), even using coercion [3] to enforce the lockdown. There were no year 2020 predictions that came close to the magnitude of devastation caused by the outbreak of the coronavirus disease that was

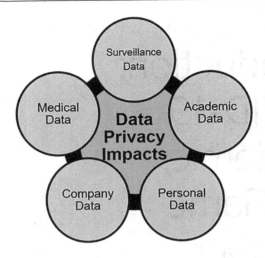

FIGURE 1.1 Impacts of COVID-19 on data privacy.

later renamed COVID-19 and classified as a pandemic by the World Health Organization.

Cybersecurity was one of the most affected fields with lots of panic-induced loopholes, conspiracies [4], cyber errors, and negligence, resulting in escalated spates of cybercrime and the consequential compromise of corporate information, loss of data, and privacy breaches across several industries. As the COVID-19 devastation on the world economy was monumental, so also were the financial and qualitative costs on the cyberspace unprecedented.

In particular, concerns over the impacts of the pandemic on data privacy [5] cut across multiple domains as depicted in Figure 1.1.

1.2 OVERVIEW OF CYBERSECURITY

As a specialized field of Information and Communications Technology (ICT), Cybersecurity focuses on protecting digital assets from various sources of threat, while preventing unauthorized modification and illegal access of data at rest, in transit or undergoing processing.

Originally, Cybersecurity deals with all the technical, administrative, and physical measures that are applied to preserve the confidentiality of information, the integrity of data and the availability of information systems used to process data. Interruptions in these areas were a key consequence of

COVID-19, accounting for over 70% of the pandemic's impact on civilization via coordinated attacks on digital operations across industries.

The fallout of the pandemic resulted in many interventions that triggered compulsory adoption of technology to fill the gaps, thereby posing a challenge to the Cybersecurity issues that arose. Notable among them was the WFH concept that became a veritable target of cyberattacks as most organizations had weak security controls that made their workforce ill-prepared to cope with the scope and pattern of the cyberattacks. Three key focus areas that dominated Cybersecurity attention were:

- Prevention of cyberattacks against vulnerable digital assets and information systems.
- Detection of planned or active cyberattacks against potential targets.
- Response actions to successful cyberattacks.

As the global impact of the pandemic left memories of panic, uncertainty, and anguish, the cyberspace continued to receive a major upsurge in online activities related to COVID-19 response, coming at a time when data network operators and cloud service providers were racing to match the rise in the patronage of online technologies in response to the social distancing protocols.

The lockdown across various territories put more pressure on ICT resources as organizations (and individuals) shifted online for almost everything ranging from academic activities, religious worship and corporate information dissemination to contract signing, product launch, sporting activities, etc.

COVID-19 related cybercrimes significantly challenged Cybersecurity interventions in both sophistication and frequency.

Within the global healthcare sector, health data is generally classified as sensitive because of its relationship with life, well-being, and healthy living. It comprises of medical records and patient-related information for the management of allergies, conditions, and diseases. Poor management of heath data can potentially result in stigmatization and privacy breaches. Its valuable nature makes it highly attractive to cyber criminals who, during the COVID-19 pandemic, employed ransomware, email scams, and social engineering to target vulnerable computing infrastructure in hospitals, pharmacies, medical laboratories, health insurance organizations, and other institutions that were involved in generating, managing, or using sensitive health-related data.

COVID-19-related cybercrimes significantly challenged Cybersecurity interventions in both sophistication and frequency, resulting in various degrees of impacts upon the cyberspace.

This book reveals how COVID-19 has opened a new perspective in the worldview of Cybersecurity and reviews the major challenges usually faced by organizations in performing effective Cybersecurity interventions. There are pertinent questions the book attempts to answer:

- To what extent has Cybersecurity protected critical business data from illegal access?
- Has the ignorance or negligence of data owners aided internet fraudster to succeed with cyberattacks?
- What are the lessons to be learnt from cases of cyber breaches in the pandemic?
- Given the sophistication of these cyberattacks, which aspects of Cybersecurity need to be optimized to match the trend?

1.3 OBJECTIVES OF THE BOOK

Cybersecurity in the COVID-19 Pandemic is written for all persons desirous of optimizing their Cybersecurity knowledge for detecting, preventing and recovering from computer crimes; and is useful to individual and corporate readers who wish to update their Cybersecurity awareness, drawing lessons from socio-technical security breaches that occurred during the COVID-19 crisis to protect their digital assets from email fraud, social engineering scams, and malware attacks.

Cybersecurity in the COVID-19 Pandemic, a book for everyone, is written in a style that teaches contemporary Cybersecurity using a reflection of specific cyberattacks that occurred during the COVID-19 pandemic and their associated impacts on the cyberspace.

The book uses real incidents to illustrate the necessity for global Cybersecurity consciousness in all spheres of human endeavour. It covers the basic concepts of Cybersecurity and leaves the reader with a lasting impression of why and how COVID-19-related cyberattacks targeted vulnerable digital assets including mobile phones, computers, websites, software, servers, networks, web application portals, databases, virtual systems, etc.

The book, which is perfectly suitable for everyone that uses the cyber-space in any form, draws lessons for individuals, professionals, research-ers, scholars, corporate organizations, and the global audience who desire to embrace and sustain the Cybersecurity culture in all spheres of human endeavour including, but not limited to, healthcare, pharmaceutical, aviation, business, e-commerce, academia, transportation and logistics, real estate, construction, manufacturing, online retail, religious affairs, diplomatic rela-tions, government, industry, research, financial institutions, insurance, fit-ness, sports and recreation, hospitality, etc.

1.4 STRUCTURE OF THE BOOK

Cybersecurity in the COVID-19 Pandemic consists of eight chapters. Except Chapter One (Introduction), Chapter Two (COVID-19 Background), and Chapter Eight (Conclusion and Recommendations), each of the remain-ing chapters addresses a specific Cybersecurity concept drawing relevance from the pandemic. To optimize the reader's understanding, each chapter approaches a topic in the following order:

- A Cybersecurity concept or term is introduced, defined, and thor-oughly explained in an understandable manner. Origin is estab-lished in some cases.
- Illustrations are made alongside real examples that are drawn from a COVID-19 scenario in which the Cybersecurity concept either occurred, was applied, or was referred to.
- Illustrations are fortified with lessons drawn from the Cybersecurity concept, presented in clear terms to aid understanding by readers at various levels, and devoid of ambiguities.
- In such cases where the Cybersecurity concept being discussed is a cybercrime or a security breach that occurred during the pan-demic, the causes and the impacts are also identified and analyzed, respectively, alongside lessons learnt.

The sequence of the chapter topics is deliberately arranged in a progressive order, such that each chapter builds upon the lessons of the preceding chapter for coherence.

There is an expansive glossary and list of acronyms that provide detailed description of specific terms used within the book.

REFERENCES

1. Centre for Productivity, Centre for Productivity, pp. 1-20, June 2020. [Online]. Available: https://www.centreforproductivity.org/ [Accessed 4 July 2020].
2. S. Talukder, I. I. Sakib and Z. Talukder, "Giving up privacy for security: A survey on privacy trade-off during pandemic emergency," *International Journal on Cryptography and Information Security (IJCIS)*, vol. 10, no. 3, 2020.
3. N. Fernandes, "Economic effects of coronavirus outbreak (COVID-19) on the world economy," Social Science Research Network (SSRN), Barcelona, Spain, 2020.
4. S. Lewandowsky and J. Cook, "*The conspiracy theory handbook*," George Mason University, Fairfax, Virginia, 2020.
5. S. Talukder, "Towards Understanding Privacy Trade-off In An Epidemic," in *36th Annual Consortium for Computing Sciences in Colleges (CCSC) Eastern Conference*, Online, 2020.

COVID-19 Background

2

2.1 NATURE

The novel coronavirus disease, formally denoted as nCoV but later renamed COVID-19 by the World Health Organization (WHO), is a new strain of the larger coronavirus family (CoV) that causes illnesses ranging from the common cold to more severe diseases such as the Middle East Respiratory Syndrome (MERS-CoV) and Severe Acute Respiratory Syndrome (SARS-CoV). Prior to the pandemic, the COVID-19 strain had never been previously identified in humans [1]. Categorized as a zoonotic disease, the coronavirus pathogen is transmitted between animals and people specifically through pathogens shared with wild or domestic animals [2].

Primary mode of transmission of the virus varies as research findings advance, but direct inhalation of droplets when an infected person sneezes, talks, yells, or sings has been established.

There are also novel indications suggesting that airborne transmission [3] might be possible in enclosed spaces and poorly ventilated enclosures. Research is on-going to authenticate some of these hypotheses.

Secondary modes of transmission include direct contacts with surviving [4] droplets of the coronavirus pathogen left on isolated or shared surfaces [5] such as fingerprint biometric scanners [6] door handles, ATM keypads, stairway rails, elevator control keypads, shopping carts, currency notes, table tops, fabrics, cardboard and plastics [7], paper, machinery buttons, touch screen computer monitors, computer keyboards, touch screen phone buttons, etc.

2.2 ORIGIN

On 31st December, 2019, the Chinese National Health Commission (NHC) informed the WHO's China office of a mysterious pneumonia-like respiratory illness in Wuhan, the capital city of Central China's Hubei province with an unknown cause. Later on 7th January, 2020, after previously reporting 44 suspected patients with the mystery disease, Chinese health authorities identified and announced the novel coronavirus as the cause of the outbreak [8].

> *... the most dominant global narrative appears to associate the origin of the December 2019 wave of the novel coronavirus disease with an outdoor market in Wuhan, China.*

Following China's report of the first death linked to the novel coronavirus, a 61-year-old male with several underlying medical conditions on 9th January, 2020, the country's NHC later shared the genetic sequence [9] of the novel coronavirus with the WHO on 12th January, 2020, in which it provided information that could help other countries in testing and tracing any potentially infected persons.

Although there are numerous conflicting and unconfirmed theories [10] till date, about the origin of the virus, one of which purports that the virus might have originated from elsewhere outside of China or might even have been existing around the world unidentified prior to the Wuhan discovery in December 2019, the most dominant global narrative appears to associate the origin of the December 2019 wave of the disease with an outdoor market in Wuhan, China. However, popular opinions in Beijing that do not accept that the virus originated from China tend to argue that just because the country first reported the virus and traced many of the first cases to Wuhan, does not necessarily mean it came from there [11].

When the virus first emerged in Wuhan, China, in December 2019, even the most experienced international public health experts never anticipated that it would rapidly spread to create the worst global public health crisis in over 100 years [12]. The spread was monumental and pervasive, and most of its impacts on civilization are permanent including its Cybersecurity link.

2.3 SPREAD

On 21st January, 2020, the WHO confirmed human-to-human transmission of the virus which had spread to South Korea [13], Thailand [14], and Japan [15] and had infected a total of 222 persons including infections among healthcare workers and caregivers who had minimal knowledge of the disease transmission mode at that time.

On 30th January, 2020, the WHO declared the outbreak a Public Health Emergency of International Concern (PHEIC) [16,17] following its rapid global spread, and on 11th February, 2020, following the unabated spread to more countries and territories and the conspicuous potentials of further widespread infections, the WHO elevated its status from a health emergency to a pandemic, and renamed the disease to coronavirus disease 2019 – COVID-19 [18, 19] in a statement released by the Director General of the WHO, Tedros Adhanom Ghebreyesus explaining that "CO" stands for "corona", "VI" for "virus", and "D" for "disease", while "19" was for the year, as the outbreak was first identified in December 2019.

Labeling the outbreak as a pandemic escalated the global panic, as countries began measures to shield off its importation into and spread within their territories. Mass evacuation of nationals became rampant across the globe and rumours of imminent bother closures were rife. At that time, the total global infection statistics according to WHO Situation Report-22 [20] was merely 43,103 cases from 25 countries and territories, with China accounting for 99.083% of that figure.

Due to its rapid spread as a PHEIC, it was speculated that depending on control measures and other factors, cases may come in waves of different heights, with high waves signaling major impact, and at different intervals [12].

2.4 GLOBAL RESPONSE

In view of the urgency required to tackle the outbreak, the international community commenced mobilization to find ways to significantly accelerate the development of interventions [16] with the WHO spearheading the coordination of global health advisories based on unfolding events. An initial challenge to the global response at the time was a lack of sufficient understanding of the nature of the disease, by virtue of its novelty to humanity.

Not too long thereafter, the global response became more massive, as countries began innovative benchmarking in implementing control measures to curb spread, including national lockdown, closure of schools, ban on social gathering, prohibition of handshaking, legislative adjustments, bother closure, advisories on respiratory hygiene, quarantine of confirmed infected persons, isolation of suspected infected persons, evacuation of citizens in foreign countries, etc. The hysteria to adopt a suitable intervention created a lot of uncertainty among countries and there was globe panic that resulted in mass lockdown across countries and territories.

- On 23rd January, 2020, China had slammed a total lockdown on Wuhan district the perceived origin of the disease (and the epicentre at the time), a lockdown that would eventually last for 76 days until April 8, 2020.
- On 29th January, 2020, the US set up a White House Coronavirus Task Force, comprising of senior officials from the Department of Health and Human Services (DHHS), Centers for Disease Control (CDC), and the Department of State (DoS). It also evacuated 195 DoS employees from Wuhan, along with their families and other US citizens [21].
- On 16th March, 2020, the US issued new guidelines that would last for an initial 2 weeks, urging people to avoid social gatherings of more than 10 people and to restrict discretionary travel [22]. The Guidelines were subsequently extended through the month of April [23]. This followed the confirmation of over 4,226 infection cases that had resulted in more than 76 fatalities in 49 states [24, 25] among which New York accounted for majority of the cases, at over 25% at the time.
- On 17th March, 2020, France announced a one-month strict confinement lockdown. The period was extended twice until 11th May when it commenced its gradual easing measures amidst mixed reactions and uncertainties.
- On 25th March, 2020, India announced a 21-day lockdown, following from a one-week test run.
- On 30th March 2020, Nigeria announced an initial lockdown of 14 days in Lagos, Ogun, and its Capital City in Abuja. The lockdown in Africa's most populous country was extended by another 14 days on 13th April, at the end of which a three-phase gradual reopening strategy commenced on 4th May, reassessed on 18th May and 1st June through 29th June, 2020. Nigeria commenced domestic flight operations on 7th July, 2020.

- On 3rd June, following prolonged lockdown, Italy began a partial reopening of its economy, having suffered one of the highest cases of the virus infection after switching positions with Spain and the UK. Many other countries and territories also began phased reopening of their economies, airspace, schools, offices, religious centres, public places and businesses rather cautiously while closely monitoring infection rates, trends, and possible effects of such partial reopening.

In addition to the lockdown approach, the global response to the pandemic included several innovative interventions that were implemented differently according to country-specific indices. Each country adapted the interventions to suit its political peculiarities, geographic attachments, and socio-cultural sensitivities. However, the implementation of the interventions by countries exposed the cyberspace to cyber criminalities and triggered associated cyber threats and risks as comprehensively illustrated in details in Table 4.1.

2.5 STATISTICS

China's Wuhan city, perceived as the pandemic's epicentre, became the first place to record a zero infection rate for nearly four consecutive weeks after its initial 76 days' lockdown [26, 27], a record that resulted partly from its aggressive national strategies facilitated by digital technologies, telemedicine, and compliance with safety precautions and health advisories.

Although gradual reopening became widespread in June 2020, by the end of July more countries had started considering options to re-impose fresh lockdown [28] in parts of their territories in the wake of a sharp spike [29] in the number of COVID-19 positive cases, and the fear of a possible second wave of the pandemic. The countries [30] included Spain, Portugal, Britain [31], Philippines, India [32], Azerbaijan, Uzbekistan, Morocco, Madagascar [33], South Africa [34], Argentina, Colombia, Israel, and Australia [35, 36].

As at 18th November, 2020 when many countries had reached several stages of easing or reimposing their lockdown measures, COVID-19 had spread to 213 countries and territories around the world and 2 international conveyances with a reported total of 55,943,189 confirmed cases, a rising death toll of 1,343,379, and a recovery figure of 38,963,254 [37, 38].

2.6 LINK WITH CYBERSECURITY

Whenever a new crisis emerges, criminal actors are usually the first to exploit innocent victims in times of fear, uncertainty, and doubt [39] such as the COVID-19 pandemic that elicited so much anxiety and panic on society and business. Apart from its extraordinary impact, the pandemic also generated unique cybercrimes that affected society and business [39].

> *Every new strategy adopted or implemented to minimize the spread of the virus or to facilitate early recovery of the infected, became an opportunity for hackers to attack vulnerable systems.*

Ironically, as countries and territories were busy deploying measures to contain the pandemic, cyber criminals and computer fraudsters equally strategized on taking advantage of the raging crisis to infiltrate porous data networks and digital assets, given the spread of the virus in a typical wildfire style. Consequently, as the global impact of the pandemic grew amid greater apprehension and emotional distress, every online resource that purported to relate to the disease or the pandemic became a source of attention, even as the world kept anticipating a lasting solution, a vaccine, or curative therapy [2, 3]. Unfortunately, the emotional distress of the hard times made the potential victims even more vulnerable [40] to cyberspace exploitation in the hands of online scammers and hacking groups.

In the midst of on-going research, cyber criminals took advantage of the global panic, fear, and desperation to launch massive cyberattacks against vulnerable systems and to steal valuable confidential data using a combination of spear-phishing emails and social engineering techniques to propagate computer virus, ransomware, etc. COVID-19 related cyber breaches also included cyber bullying that was rampantly perpetrated through the dissemination of computer-aided victimization, deep fakes, unsubstantiated media claims [41], and fake news, with perpetrators hiding under the anonymity of social media and micro blogging platforms.

The link between COVID-19 and Cybersecurity is that cyber criminals including internet hackers and online fraudsters capitalized on the pandemic to launch massive computer attacks on unsuspecting victims. They stole identities and disrupted digital transactions using sophisticated versions of conventional cyberattack techniques that were specifically modified to match the pattern of COVID-19-related vulnerabilities. Cyber criminals preyed on people's heightened anxiety during the pandemic, used a combination of social engineering, phishing email scams, and ransomware, and tricked them into clicking and sharing links that stole information [42]. The adversaries simply capitalized on the pandemic environment to compromise and manipulate inadequately protected systems for their benefits.

Besides, every new strategy adopted or implemented to minimize the spread of the virus or to facilitate early recovery of the infected became an opportunity for internet hackers and online fraudsters to attack vulnerable systems and take advantage of unsuspecting cyberspace users. Essentially, cyber criminals ruthlessly exploited COVID-19 fears.

The ruthless extortion [43] of victims via public shaming, victimization, and stigmatization on account of their health status or medical condition further demonstrated the extent to which cyber criminals exploited the COVID-19 pandemic to make illicit benefit, in the process of which they equally inflicted emotional harm to computer users whose data was either stolen or their online services disrupted.

REFERENCES

1. "Coronavirus," World Health Organization (WHO). [Online]. Available: https://www.who.int/health-topics/coronavirus [Accessed 4 February 2020].
2. K. U. Okereafor and O. Adebola, "Tackling the cybersecurity impacts of the coronavirus outbreak as a challenge to internet safety," *International Journal in IT and Engineering (IJITE)*, vol. 8, no. 2, pp. 1–14, 2020.
3. R. Zhang, Y. Li, A. L. Zhang, Y. Wang and M. J. Molina, "Identifying airborne transmission as the dominant route for the spread of COVID-19," *Proceedings of the National Academy of Sciences (PNAS) of the United States of America*, vol. 117, no. 26, pp. 14857–14863, 2020.
4. A. Krammer and O. Assadian, "*Survival of microorganisms on inanimate surfaces: Use of biocidal surfaces for reduction of healthcare acquired infections*," Springer, Switzerland, 2014.
5. K. U. Okereafor, O. Adebola and R. Djehaiche, "Exploring the potentials of telemedicine and other non-contact electronic health technologies in controlling the spread of the novel Coronavirus disease (COVID-19)," *International Journal in IT & Engineering*, vol. 8, no. 4, pp. 1–11, 2020.
6. K. Okereafor, I. Ekong, I. O. Markson and K. Enwere, "Fingerprint biometric system hygiene and the risk of COVID-19 transmission," *Journal of Medical Internet Research (JMIR) Biomededical Engineering (BME)*, 2020. [Online]. Available: https://biomedeng.jmir.org/2020/1/e19623/. doi: 10.2196/19623

7. L. Siroli, F. Patrignani, D. I. Serrazanetti, C. Chiavari, M. Benevelli, L. Grazia and R. Lanciotti, "Survival of spoilage and pathogenic microorganisms on cardboard and plastic packaging materials," *Frontiers in Microbiology*, vol. 8, p. 2606, 2017.

8. J. L. Ravelo and S. Jerving, "COVID-19 — a timeline of the coronavirus outbreak," DEVEX, 25 May 2020. [Online]. Available: https://www.devex.com/news/covid-19-a-timeline-of-the-coronavirus-outbreak-96396 [Accessed 25 May 2020].

9. World Health Organization, "Novel Coronavirus – China," World Health Organization, 12 January 2020. [Online]. Available: https://www.who.int/csr/don/12-january-2020-novel-coronavirus-china/en/ [Accessed 25 May 2020].

10. S. Lewandowsky and J. Cook, *The Conspiracy Theory Handbook*, George Mason University, Fairfax, Virginia, 2020.

11. Kathy Gilsinan, "How China is planning to win back the world," The Atlantic, 28 May 2020. [Online]. Available: https://www.theatlantic.com/politics/archive/2020/05/china-disinformation-propaganda-united-states-xi-jinping/612085/ [Accessed 18 August 2020].

12. K. A. Moore, M. Lipsitch, J. M. Barry and M. T. Osterholm, *COVID-19: The CIDRAP Viewpoint. Part 1: The future of the COVID-19 pandemic: Lessons learned from pandemic influenza,* Center for Infectious Disease Research and Policy (CIDRP), University of Minnesota, Minnesota, 2020.

13. World Health Organization, "First meeting of Emergency Committee regarding the novel coronavirus outbreak," World Health Organization, 23 January 2020. [Online]. Available: https://www.who.int/emergencies/diseases/novel-coronavirus-2019/events-as-they-happen [Accessed 25 May 2020].

14. World Health Organization, "WHO statement on novel coronavirus in Thailand," World Health Organization, 13 January 2020. [Online]. Available: https://www.who.int/news/item/13-01-2020-who-statement-on-novel-coronavirus-in-thailand [Accessed 25 May 2020].

15. World Health Organization, "Novel Coronavirus – Japan (ex-China)," World Health Organization, 17 January 2020. [Online]. Available: https://www.who.int/csr/don/17-january-2020-novel-coronavirus-japan-ex-china/en/ [Accessed 25 May 2020].

16. World Health Organization, "COVID-19 Public Health Emergency of International Concern (PHEIC) Global research and innovation forum," World Health Organization, 12 February 2020. [Online]. Available: https://www.who.int/who-documents-detail/covid-19-public-health-emergency-of-international-concern-(PHEIC)-global-research-and-innovation-forum [Accessed 25 May 2020].

17. World Health Organization, "COVID 19 Public Health Emergency of International Concern (PHEIC) Global research and innovation forum: towards a research roadmap," World Health Organization R&D Blueprint: Global Research Collaboration for Infectious Disease Preparedness, Geneva, 2020.

18. S. Jiang, Z. Shi, Y. Shu, J. Song, G. F. Gao, W. Tan and D. Guo, "A distinct name is needed for the new coronavirus," *The Lancet Journal*, vol. 395, no. 10228, p. 949, 2020.

19. World Health Organization, "Naming the coronavirus disease (COVID-19) and the virus that causes it," 11 February 2020. [Online]. Available: https://www.who.int/emergencies/diseases/novel-coronavirus-2019/technical-guidance/naming-the-coronavirus-disease-(covid-2019)-and-the-virus-that-causes-it [Accessed 14 May 2020].

20. World Health Organization, "Novel Coronavirus (2019-nCoV) Situation Report – 22," World Health Organization, Geneva, 2020.

21. E. Beech and S. Gorman, "Two more U.S. evacuation planes leave coronavirus epicenter Wuhan," Reuters, 7 January 2020. [Online]. Available: https://web.archive.org/web/20200216045906/https://www.reuters.com/article/us-china-health-usa/two-planes-left-wuhan-china-en-route-to-us-state-department-idUSKBN20105M [Accessed 25 May 2020].

22. K. Rogers and E. Cochrane, "Trump Urges Limits Amid Pandemic, But Stops Short of National Mandates," New York Times, 16 March 2020. [Online]. Available: https://www.nytimes.com/2020/03/16/us/politics/trump-coronavirus-guidelines.html [Accessed 25 May 2020].

23. R. Goodman and D. Schulkin, "Timeline of the Coronavirus Pandemic and U.S. Response," Just Security, 7 February 2020. [Online]. Available: https://www.justsecurity.org/69650/timeline-of-the-coronavirus-pandemic-and-u-s-response/ [Accessed 25 May 2020].

24. Morbidity & Mortality Weekly Report, "Severe Outcomes Among Patients With Coronavirus Disease 2019 (COVID-19) — United States, February 12–March 16, 2020," Medscape. [Online]. Available: https://www.medscape.com/viewarticle/927663 [Accessed 25 May 2020].

25. "Cumulative cases of COVID-19 in the U.S. from January 22 to May 24, 2020, by day," Statista, 24 MAy 2020. [Online]. Available: https://www.statista.com/statistics/1103185/cumulative-coronavirus-covid19-cases-number-us-by-day/ [Accessed 25 May 2020].

26. Medical Xpress, "China's ground zero reports virus infections (Update)," Medical Xpress, 10 May 2020. [Online]. Available: https://medicalxpress.com/news/2020-05-china-wuhan-virus-infection-month.html [Accessed 25 May 2020].

27. World Health Organization, "Report of the WHO-China Joint Mission on Coronavirus Disease 2019 (COVID-19)," World Health Organization, Geneva, 2020.

28. P. Beaumont, "Global report: Cities worldwide reimpose lockdowns as Covid-19 cases surge," The Guardian, 14 July 2020. [Online]. Available: https://www.theguardian.com/world/2020/jul/14/global-wrap-cities-worldwide-reimpose-lockdowns-as-covid-19-cases-surge [Accessed 14 August 2020].

29. S. R. Apparasu, "Telangana likely to reimpose lockdown in Hyderabad, surroundings as Covid-19 cases surge," Hindustan Times, 28 June 2020. [Online]. Available: https://www.hindustantimes.com/india-news/telangana-likely-to-reimpose-lockdown-in-hyderabad-and-surroundings-as-covid-cases-spike/story-ch34ShtPSM4ljUGq4LnDuO.html [Accessed 14 August 2020].

30. Countries that were forced to re-impose local lockdowns to curb surge in COVID-19 cases," Wio News, June 2020. [Online]. Available: https://www.wionews.com/photos/countries-that-were-forced-to-re-impose-local-lockdowns-to-curb-surge-in-covid-19-cases-313088#europe-301206 [Accessed 14 August 2020].

31. "Britain reimposes lockdown on English city of Leicester after coronavirus spike," Los Angeles Times, 30 June 2020. [Online]. Available: https://www. latimes.com/world-nation/story/2020-06-30/britain-reimposes-lockdown-leicester-after-coronavirus-spike [Accessed 14 August 2020].

32. "Covid-19: Authorities re-impose lockdown in Srinagar," Deccan Herald, 12 July 2020. [Online]. Available: https://www.deccanherald.com/national/north-and-central/covid-19-authorities-re-impose-lockdown-in-srinagar-860179.html [Accessed 14 August 2020].

33. "Madagascar re-imposes lockdown amid surge in virus cases," The Jakarta Post, Agence France-Presse, 6 July 2020. [Online]. Available: https://www. thejakartapost.com/news/2020/07/06/madagascar-re-imposes-lockdown-amid-surge-in-virus-cases.html [Accessed 14 August 2020].

34. F. Miller, "South Africa reimposes lockdown amid soaring COVID-19 cases," Al Jazeera, 13 July 2020. [Online]. Available: https://www.aljazeera.com/news/2020/07/south-africa-reimposes-lockdown-soaring-covid-19-cases-200713182836729.html [Accessed 14 August 2020].

35. N. Gan and A. Watson, "Australia to reimpose six-week coronavirus lockdown in second largest city as country battles potential second wave," CNN, 7 July 2020. [Online]. Available: https://edition.cnn.com/2020/07/07/asia/melbourne-coronavirus-lockdown-intl-hnk/index.html [Accessed 14 August 2020].

36. A recurring nightmare: Australia reimposes lockdown amid fears of second wave of coronavirus," Wio News, July 2020. [Online]. Available: https://www. wionews.com/photos/a-recurring-nightmare-australia-reimposes-lockdown-amid-fears-of-second-wave-of-coronavirus-311906#new-lockdown-311887 [Accessed 14 August 2020].

37. "WHO Coronavirus Disease (COVID-19) dashboard," World Health Organization, 18th November 2020. [Online]. Available: https://covid19.who. int/ [Accessed 18th November 2020].

38. Coronavirus Cases," Worldometers, 18th November 2020. [Online]. Available: https://www.worldometers.info/coronavirus/ [Accessed 18th November 2020].

39. United Nations Office on Drugs & Crime (UNODC), "COVID-19: Cyber threat analysis," Cybercrime Program, UNODC Middle East and North Africa (MENA) Assessment & Actions, Cairo, 2020.

40. P. Passeri, "1-15 May 2020 cyber attacks timeline," HACKMAGEDDON: Information security timelines and statistics, 19 June 2020. [Online]. Available: https://www.hackmageddon.com/2020/06/19/1-15-may-2020-cyber-attacks-timeline/ [Accessed 30 July 2020].

41. "China coronavirus: Misinformation spreads online about origin and scale," BBC Trending, 30 January 2020. [Online]. Available: https://www.bbc.com/news/blogs-trending-51271037 [Accessed 11 February 2020].

42. J. Tidy, "Honda's global operations hit by cyber-attack," BBC News, 9 June 2020. [Online]. Available: https://www.bbc.com/news/technology-52982427 [Accessed 19 August 2020].

43. Security Lab, "Clop, Clop! It's a TA505 HTML malspam analysis," Hornet Security, 7 July 2020. [Online]. Available: https://www.hornetsecurity.com/en/security-information/clop-clop-ta505-html-malspam-analysis/#:":text=the%20Clop%20ransomware.-,Clop%20ransomware,stage%20of%20an%20TA505%20attack [Accessed 28 July 2020].

Cybersecurity Roles in a Pandemic

3

From inception, expectations are usually high on the ability of Cybersecurity to guarantee a safe cyberspace particularly in the face of disruptions due to the pandemic. A pandemic on its own neither stops nor promotes cybercrime activities but can potentially trigger a chain of abnormal events that could lead to elevated waves of cybercrimes. This domino effect scenario played out completely in the COVID-19 pandemic.

The pandemic created an opportunity for individuals and organizations to examine their digital assets and become more conscious of the security impacts on their infrastructure.

It was the rise in cybercrime cases that eventually ignited the focus on Cybersecurity interventions, with an emphasis not only to track indicators of compromise (IoC) but also to mitigate the impacts of cyber breaches as much as possible. Consequently, the global demand for Cybersecurity in organizations and private computing has significantly risen more than ever, and in the next 30 years, Cybersecurity will remain the most sought-after career globally [1].

Given the effect of the pandemic on increased patronage for online services and resources, the Cybersecurity expectations were justifiable, ranging from supporting the adherence to cyberspace ethics to mitigating data breaches whose occurrence could be traceable to societal actions, reactions, and inactions to the life style adjustments imposed for dealing with the pandemic itself. Much of COVID-19 incidents mirrored the patterns of people either starting to work from home in compliance with the lockdown advisories or undertaking some detrimental reactionary actions while adhering to the requirements of the social distancing protocols.

In the first instance, the fundamental focus of Cybersecurity never shifted from addressing issues of protection of the data life cycle from its creation to disposal. Expectations were hinged on holistic data protection in the following three instances:

- Proactively: For example, by using a well-configured firewall or other *preventive* countermeasures to intercept cyberattack patterns before they end up infiltrating the data network and circumventing digital assets leading to undesirable outcomes.
- Instantaneously: For example, by applying an Intrusion Detection System or other *detective* countermeasures to spot spam emails at the time of occurrence in the mail server, or to identify other hostile network traffic patterns indicative of a cyberattack.
- Retroactively: For example, by using incident management, forensics, and other *response* countermeasures to audit, reconstruct, and investigate an incident after it has occurred.

On the other hand, the pandemic created an opportunity for individuals and organizations to see beyond the ordinary, examine their digital assets, identify network hiccups, detect storage deficiencies, and become more conscious of the security impacts on their infrastructure. While data lifecycle management was imperative, the operating environments and nature of infrastructure within which data was to be processed or transmitted, respectively, needed major attention.

The combination of these was all that was needed to provide justification for the preventive, detective, and response roles of *Cybersecurity in the COVID-19 pandemic*.

3.1 PREVENTIVE ROLES

A major role of Cybersecurity is the *prevention* of potential harm or actual damage to data and digital resources. By extension, this role includes protection of data processing systems, protection of the people that manage the data, as well as safeguarding the environment around which data resides or passes through while being processed.

During the pandemic, preventive roles were particularly anticipated in determining the risks to online data and privacy across several cyberspace services through proactive privacy impact assessment, a role that suffered peculiar setbacks as a result of the pandemic's anxieties and uncertainties. Three components of the assessment were in focus as follows:

- Actual risks arising from the specifics of the system or service [2].
- Threats existing due to the scope of the service.
- Vulnerabilities in the technology employed and how the technology is used.

Cybersecurity also includes the best practices, policies, standards, and frameworks that protect corporate applications and data from being threatened by threat actors. These provide guidance for regulation and protection at multiple levels. At the peak of the COVID-19 crises, just when network intrusion prevention was in high demand, the expectation was that all pre-existing preventive measures would come to play to offer superior data loss prevention (DLP) roles to forestall threats in various forms. Anticipated threats included email fraud, identity theft, wireless network hijack, database attack, distributed denial of service (DDoS), man-in-the-middle attack, remote communications hiccups, espionage, etc.

3.2 DETECTIVE ROLES

It is often said in the security domain that *"prevention is ideal, but detection is a must"* [3]. It is impracticable to guarantee and attain 100% absolute prevention of threat actions due to many factors including the dynamic nature of the threat landscape in addition to the ever-changing superiority of the adversary's attack power. For this reason, a standard proactive approach in the industry is the use of detection and alert systems.

This was a particularly suitable and preferred approach during the pandemic given that top-notch internal defenses could not be substantially guaranteed under such chaotic circumstances where much emphasis was on staying alive at the expense of maintaining online safety. This approach called for adequate threat identification using security tools and emergency management methodologies to identify active security threats in advance. Internet hackers capitalized on the sense of urgency knowing that there was limited time for people to act amidst weak defenses over remote networks. Proactive detection was in focus since cyberattackers generally follow specific steps to launch an attack, avoid detection, and dig deeper into a compromised system [4].

In the process of attacking a system and evading detection, the adversary procedurally exploits a vulnerable user or a porous endpoint, conceals self, and establishes a back door while remaining as stealth as possible. In an ideal situation, all the attacker's abnormal behaviour, also known as events of interest (EoI) or IoC should be anticipated, quickly detected, analyzed, and appropriate actions taken, but the peculiarities of the pandemic jeopardized every adherence to the ideal, for most users.

Detective actions that could be taken in response to EoI and IoC include eliminating threats, identifying, and remediating sources of vulnerabilities, and repairing systems through updated patches. In just the same way that operating systems need to be up to date and fully patched, endpoint security also requires automatic updates on a regular basis [5] to fulfil their detective roles.

3.3 RESPONSE ROLES

Cybersecurity operations are incomplete without a deliberate plan for responding to incidents, assuming the preventive and detective roles are unable to stop or identify active threats owing to superior attack power.

. Response roles are activated if both prevention and detection are unable to intercept or repel a cyberattack. They are put in place as threat remedies to respond to the resulting threat incident by taking mitigation actions to minimize the possibility of further attacks, reduce its impact, lower its spread, as well as facilitate early recovery from such disaster. Threat remedies isolate or contain threats using strategies and tools that reduce the impact of active security threats, especially those that have already gone beyond corporate security defenses and penetrated the data network.

In exercising these preventive, detective, and response roles, Cybersecurity offers three categories of such protection over data, namely:

- Protection from unauthorized access to data, also known as confidentiality protection.
- Protection from illegal modification of data, also known as integrity protection.
- Protection from delays in accessing data by authorized persons, also known as availability protection.

These three categories of data protection are collectively referred to as CIA triad (i.e. Confidentiality, Integrity, and Availability, respectively). The CIA triad is a model that provides direction for the development, formulation, and maintenance of information security policies within corporate organizations or among individual users. It guides organizations and persons on how to keep their sensitive data secure while at rest, in motion, or in process. To avoid confusing the model's acronym with the Central Intelligence Agency, it is also sometimes referred to as the AIC triad (i.e. Availability, Integrity, and Confidentiality).

The CIA triad is very essential to providing protection for data throughout its life cycle. Figure 3.1 shows the data life cycle's dependence on the CIA upon which data draws relevance for protection at each stage.

As the phases of data life cycle are illustrated as clusters surrounding the CIA triad, so does each phase depend completely on the CIA for all round protection.

- *Data creation phase*

  Data creation or generation is achieved either by acquisition from a pre-existing external source or by first-hand onboarding via direct capture. For example, direct biometric capture of personal data of a potential health insurance enrollee, export of citizen's identities from the bank customer database into the national identity repository via data harmonization.

  Data creation through any means is expected to satisfy Cybersecurity requirements of privacy and confidentiality by using best practices that do not unduly expose personal records to unauthorized persons. This involves focusing on initial creation of

FIGURE 3.1   Data life cycle protected by the CIA triad.

data based on the appropriate level of trust for a first-time interaction [6] whether by acquisition or onboarding.

Biometric-based data has the ability to uniquely identify humans [7] and, therefore, it is a necessary expectation that the creation process for every biometric information must conform to global standards [8, 9], while meeting specifications for detecting and preventing unauthorized modification [10], alteration, or outright deletion [11–14].

By ensuring that processes adopted for creating data and establishing digital identities follow standards and best practices, there is a guarantee that such data when used in subsequent authentication and identity proofing of individuals can be fully trusted.

- *Data collation phase*

  Data collation entails arranging or stacking data in such a systematic manner as to produce meaningful information that can facilitate analytics and decision making. Classifying data in a systematic and secure manner is as important a process as generating them because poor classification could trigger issues with inaccessibility that could compromise availability and equally place confidentiality and integrity in jeopardy.

  Data classification when considered at the collation phase categorizes data based on relevance, criticality, and value, without which it becomes problematic to determine the level of Cybersecurity investment that must be bestowed to a digital asset to ensure its CIA [15]. Data collation via classification ensures that a digital asset hosting critical data of immense business value is accorded superior surveillance to preserve its integrity and guarantee its availability at all times.

From a data protection point of view, after the creation and collation of identities, some key security questions in the minds of users require attention as follows:

- What is the data intended for?
- Who will have access to the data?
- Do users have a choice to control how, when, and with whom they give access to their data?
- How will the data be disposed of?

Addressing these questions was a major challenge during the COVID-19 pandemic as they bothered on trust, sincerity, clarity, openness, believability, accuracy, honesty, and fairness; all of which required a combination of good data security ethics, resilient policies, and investment in appropriate Cybersecurity technologies. Unfortunately, the desperation of the moment made every coordinated approach a mirage, as the priority attention was to save human lives and contain the spread of the disease.

- *Data transmission phase*

  Data transmission phase takes care of various connectivity options for the purpose of communicating, sharing, or exchanging data securely using standard protocols. Standards for the secure transmission of data rely on encryption protocols including but not limited to Secure Sockets Layer (SSL), Transport Layer Security (TLS), and many others.

- *Data sharing and communication phase*

  COVID-19 impacted on the secure exchange of data across beneficiaries and stakeholders, resulting in operational disruption and occasional loss. Digital data is usually exchanged among beneficiaries using several technologies to facilitate speed and reliability in querying, retrieving, and visualizing data in varying forms.

  At such a critical time as the COVID-19 crisis, the CIA triad expectedly would play a crucial role as electronic data traversed across networks in the form of medical statistics on disease spread, logistics on test kits, fatality rates, and related data.

- *Data security and storage phase*

  The preservation of data integrity entails the deployment of appropriate tools and enabling ICT governance policies to secure data at each stage (at rest, in storage, in transit, and under processing).

  Commensurate protective measures are assigned to safeguard data confidentiality, privacy, and secrecy as appropriate. These measures are accomplished with the aid of security tools and adherence to global best practices in privacy. The storage phase takes care of data use and ethics and the application of periodic updates by authorized parties.

- *Data disposal phase*

  Depending on an organization's data retention policy concerning archived data, disposal by destruction becomes inevitable at some point in order to free up storage space and accommodate fresh data entries. A deliberate policy, specific to the organization, guides the destruction of unwanted and outdated data in digital form following global best practices for disposal of digital media such as degaussing, counter magnetization, and shredding.

To properly understand the depth of data protection expected as Cybersecurity roles during the pandemic, it is important to associate each of the discussed phases of the data life cycle above with the concept of the CIA triad.

The *confidentiality* of classified medical data and sensitive health records moving across networks between isolation centres and medical laboratories needed to be protected from eavesdroppers, just as critical health information required *integrity* assurances and superior protection from all forms of illegitimate alterations, both of which could cause delayed access even to authorized persons and compromise their *availability*. COVID-19 witnessed several security breaches that cut cross across these three attributes: confidentiality, integrity, and availability.

3.4 DATA CONFIDENTIALITY

As the pandemic rolled along and as information maintained its dynamism, data confidentiality roles became increasingly more demanding as an integral part of cyberspace safety and digital protection. Confidentiality is the assurance that data is not made accessible to authorized persons and that what is communicated is safe from unauthorized disclosure, from end to end. Poor confidentiality exposes sensitive and private data of victims to unauthorized persons and services.

As the most obvious security aspect of the CIA triad, confidentiality provides the ability to hide information from the view of unauthorized parties. It is perhaps the most attacked, as it is threatened by espionage and data theft from cyber criminals. Encryption provides a technical measure for ensuring the confidentiality of data transferred from one computer to another, or across multiple networks such as over the internet.

3.5 DATA INTEGRITY

The integrity of data refers to the assurance that it is not modified in an unauthorized manner or by unauthorized persons and means. Harm to data integrity was a major threat to businesses during the COVID-19 pandemic whereby electronic information assets that fell victims to cyberattacks suffered various forms of unauthorized modification in content and illegal manipulations in context.

Data integrity assures that data is an accurate representation from its original, by assessing whether it has been compromised with malicious or unauthorized codes. Anything that potentially alters the originality of information through illegitimate means, compromises its integrity. Integrity checkers preserve privacy and ensure consent by preventing illegal manipulation or alteration of data.

3.6 DATA AVAILABILITY

Data is said to be available when it is freely accessible to authorized parties without delays, hiccups, and difficulties. As the COVID-19 pandemic lasted, isolated incidents of data theft and privacy breaches naturally led to availability challenges. Denial of service and data deletion attacks threatened availability. For example, the accessibility difficulties that are generally encountered in a ransomware case when the adversary locks an electronic file, a computer terminal, or online resource through encryption in expectation of ransom while threatening deletion or exposure.

Availability component of the data creation phase is maintained by putting measures to ensure that data access is not hindered by technical or system-related hiccups such as slow retrieval codes and internet speed limitations. From a security viewpoint, it is essential that information is readily accessible to the authorized party to prevent escalated consequences. For example, by denying access to a hijacked website, a hacking group could appear popular or seem to be propagating a certain ideology by instilling psychological trauma associated with the attack.

3.7 CHAPTER SUMMARY

The pattern of COVID-19 related cybercrimes left huge consequences on the confidentiality of data, the integrity of information, and the availability of systems.

Cybercrime has been a major threat to global economics [16] and digital commerce. When unchecked, cyber criminalities directly affect individual safety and the well-being of the general public, and it remains a potential medium that can fuel radical and ideological actions such as asymmetric warfare and terrorism. The impacts of cybercrime impose grievous consequences on both individual and corporate organizations.

The pattern of COVID-19-related cybercrimes clearly left huge consequences on the *confidentiality* of data in addition to the *integrity* of information and the *availability* of the systems that process data. An understanding of the CIA triad and the impacts its relegation can exert on the cyberspace are essential ingredients to protect information flow from its creation through storage to the time when it becomes obsolete and is eventually destroyed through an appropriate technique such as deletion.

The CIA triad is applicable across a wide range of practical scenarios including to checkmate attacker's action of accessing a user's internet history, securing encrypted data across the cyberspace, and verifying that an electronic message remains unchanged while in transit or storage. A breach in any of the three CIA components can result in far-reaching impacts on the other two, and in extreme cases, can cause serious security concerns for the parties involved.

A review of COVID-19 incidents affecting the CIA components reveals the vacuum created when there is no balance between preventive, detective, and response roles. This revelation helps in avoiding compliance issues, ensures business continuity, and prevents reputational damage to individuals and organizations, all of which are fallouts of active Cybersecurity breaches.

REFERENCES

1. E. Cole, "VIRTUAL CISO," Secure Anchor, 2020. [Online]. Available: https://safe.secure-anchor.com/vciso-ws [Accessed 9 June 2020].
2. M. Paul, "Digital identity: Issue analysis," Consult Hyperion, New York, 2016.
3. E. Cole, Composer, *SANS GSEC Cybersecurity Essential Tutorial*. [Sound Recording]. SANS Institute. 2010.
4. E. Cole, Threat hunting. What is it, who's doing it, and how to get started yourself, Secure Anchor Consulting, Ashburn, Virginia, 2020.
5. E. Cole, "*PHISHING: You are a target*," Secure Anchor Consulting, Ashburn, VA, 2020.
6. D. Black, "How to accelerate digital identity in the UK," Computer Weekly, 31 January 2019. [Online]. Available: https://www.computerweekly.com/opinion/How-to-accelerate-digital-identity-in-the-UK [Accessed 17 May 2020].
7. C. U. Ebelogu, O. E. Amujo, O. I. Adelaiye and A. S. Faki, "Privacy concerns in biometrics," *IEEE SEM*, vol. 10, no. 7, pp. 45–52, 2019.

8. P. Grother, W. Salamon and R. Chandramouli, *"Biometric specifications for personal identity verification: NIST special publication 800-76-2,"* National Institute of Standards and Technology (NIST, Maryland, 2013.

9. C. Tilton, *"Biometric standards – An overview,"* Daon Inc, Dublin, Ireland, 2006.

10. K. Stine, R. Kissel, W. C. Barker, J. Fahlsing and J. Gulick, *"Volume I: Guide for mapping types of information and information systems to security categories,"* National Institute of Standards and Technology (NIST), Maryland, 2008.

11. "United Nations Compendium of recommended practices for the responsible use and sharing of biometrics in counter-terrorism," United Nations Office of Counter Terrorism, New York, 2018.

12. M. Tracy, W. Jansen, K. Scarfone and J. Butterfield, *"NIST guidelines on electronic mail security,"* National Institute of Standards and Technology (NIST) Maryland, 2007.

13. SANS Institute, *"Password Construction Guidelines,"* SANS Institute, Maryland, 2017.

14. SANS Institute, *"Password Protection Policy,"* SANS Institute, Maryland, USA, 2017.

15. K. Okereafor and R. Djehaiche, "New approaches to the application of digital forensics in cybersecurity: A proposal," *International Journal of Simulation: Systems, Science and Technology (IJSSST)*, vol. 21, no. 2, pp. 36.1–36.6, 2020.

16. W. Lee and B. Rotoloni, *"Emerging Cyber Threats Report 2016,"* Institute for Information Security and Privacy (IISP), Georgia Institute of Technology, Atlanta, 2016.

Cyberspace at Risk

4

No business is completely immune from the risk of cyberattacks, and as the COVID-19 pandemic raged on, the cyber risk patterns and exposures became more apparent.

During the COVID-19 pandemic, vulnerabilities manifested mainly as unknown flaws and weaknesses that attackers took advantage of, to compromise corporate data privacy and sensitive personal information.

With the passage of time, it became obvious that each good-intentioned global intervention to contain the spread of the virus was in some way exploited by malicious hackers and internet fraudsters using hostile exploits to initiate a unique type of cyberattack on the cyberspace, thereby increasing risks of data loss, identity theft, and operational disruption.

From quarantine and lockdown to work from home, cyber criminals saw every intervention as a potential accessory to perpetrate online crimes, as they were quick to figure out ways to circumvent it to their advantage, as if they never ran out of ideas. The risk factors especially on privacy were simply unlimited, so were the consequences.

Table 4.1 provides a listing of COVID-19 interventions alongside the Cybersecurity risks associated with each of them at the time.

Table 4.1 is a generalized listing showing the respective threats and risks arising from specific COVID-19 remedial interventions. Although the scope and timing of each cyber threat and the resulting breach differed by location during the pandemic, the impacts of successful breaches were huge and equally varied by case, background, and circumstances.

Potentially, breaches [1], or human or technological errors could result in any or combination of these:

TABLE 4.1 Cybersecurity threats and risks associated with COVID-19 interventions

INTERVENTION		DESCRIPTION	ASSOCIATED CYBER THREATS AND RISKS
Medical	Quarantine	Restriction of movement of confirmed infected person(s) to prevent retransmission of COVID-19.	Spear phishing email, cloned website, cyber espionage, ransomware, password cracking and dictionary attack, computer virus, other malware, phone scam, etc.
	Contact tracing	Tracking and finding all persons suspected to have had close contact with a confirmed or suspected infected person(s).	Cyber bullying, cyberstalking, ransomware, impersonation, phone hacking, website hijacking, spear phishing email, social engineering, adware, etc.
	Isolation	Separation of suspected infected person(s) from social interaction, to control exposure.	Cyber espionage, malware, man-in-the-middle attack, etc.
	Rapid testing	Establishment of diagnostic and testing centres.	Social engineering, Trojan horse, ransomware, spear phishing email, adware, spyware, etc.

Social	Lockdown	Imposition of movement restrictions to slow down infection rates within a neighbourhood, county, state, region, or country.	Teleworking exploit, man-in-the-middle attack, eavesdropping, interception of video conferencing, zoom-bombing on virtual meeting session, identity theft on social networking website, social engineering, confidence trick, phone prank, etc.
	Social gathering ban and social distancing	Limiting of person-to-person proximity and crowd control to minimize the infection rate.	Spear phishing email, website hijacking, social engineering, cloned website, cyber bullying, etc.
	Border closure and travel ban	Restriction of movement of persons across different territorial borders to prevent importation of the disease.	
Personal	Wearing of face masks and shields	Imposition of face covering in public places to curtail transmission of the virus and control the infection rates.	Impersonation, adware, fake news, obscenity, confidence trick, cloned website, social engineering, shoulder surfing, spear phishing, cyber bullying, cyberstalking, ransomware, etc.
	Hand hygiene	Enforcement of handwashing and sanitization culture.	
	Ban on handshaking	Enforcement of "no handshake" policy.	

- Unauthorized access to, disclosure, modification, misuse, loss, or destruction of company, customer, or other third-party data and systems.
- Theft of sensitive, regulated, or confidential data, including personal information and intellectual property.
- The loss of access to critical data and systems due to ransomware, or disruptive attacks.
- Business delays, service or system disruptions, or denials of service.

Selected threats, exploits, and cyber breaches are discussed below under specific headings. Each heading is defined, explained, and illustrated with reference to its COVID-19 relevance, to aid understanding.

4.1 VULNERABILITIES AND EXPOSURES

4.1.1 Vulnerabilities

A vulnerability is any weakness or flaw in a computer system which, if left unresolved, could expose the system to potential dangers, or increase the risks of possible cyberattacks, and could be exploited by a threat to cause harm or undesirable consequences. A vulnerability represents a weakness in the system that is capable of giving the threat agent the opportunity to compromise [2] part of, or the entire system.

During the COVID-19 pandemic, vulnerabilities manifested mainly as unknown flaws and weaknesses in digital resources, which posed varied levels of risks that attackers took advantage of to circumvent the system. The desperate and urgent manner of responding to COVID-19's medical, social, and personal interventions around the globe, as illustrated in Table 4.1, gave rise to different types of vulnerabilities in technology, digital behaviour [3], and the human factor, all of which contributed greatly to the alarming rate of Cybersecurity challenges experienced at the time of the crisis.

4.1.2 Exposures

An exposure is a measure of the extent to which a threat and vulnerability can both combine to place the system at risk of cyberattack, leading to an actual compromise or exploit. The key reasons that fueled the rise in cybercrime incidents in the COVID-19 pandemic were people's online behaviour, anxiety to access the updated information on the disease, as well as inadequately-protected data networks exacerbated by unprecedented remote work limitations [4].

Ordinarily, there are numerous exposures to which online information systems and the data they protect are exposed to in the cyberspace, but an exposed system is a potential target of attack by virtue of the presence of the vulnerability. A vulnerable system becomes attractive to the cyber criminal, who has several tools and threats at his disposal to exploit any unmitigated weakness and launch an attack. Every Cybersecurity breach is a typical product of a threat that has taken advantage of exposure to a known or unknown vulnerability to launch a cyberattack, resulting in a quantifiable impact.

While a system may possess vulnerabilities, if the threat exposure is only limited, then the overall risk may be low [2]. Conversely, a vulnerable system that is surrounded by many threats in the form of robust use of technology in scale and scope such as experienced during the pandemic becomes a target of great interest to the cyber criminals, resulting in higher risks of attack.

4.1.3 Exposed Industries

Although the rate of exposure to Cybersecurity exploits was pervasive during the pandemic, certain industries and sectors were evidently more prone to the actual data security breaches than the others due to their direct involvement in managing the pandemic's data or because of the value attached to the category of data they generated, managed, or had custody of.

Healthcare institutions were the most vulnerable targets of attack in terms of the commercial benefits to the attackers and the potential impacts a compromise would make. The institutions were involved in generating, using, or managing sensitive healthcare data requiring high levels of confidentiality and privacy which made them valuable assets, attractive to the hackers.

Healthcare institutions, in this category, included hospitals, medical research institutes, pharmaceutical companies, medical supplies and logistics, health maintenance organizations, medical laboratories, health insurance operators, medical manufacturing companies, health education institutions, private health regulators, government health regulators, health funders, and digital health organizations.

Other exposed industries were hi-tech companies, financial institutions, eCommerce organizations, social networking organizations, and transportation companies due to their potentials of wider coverage and larger user base.

Given the spate of cyberattacks during the pandemic, and the level of exposure exhibited by the most vulnerable systems, the following vulnerabilities were widespread.

4.2 HUMAN VULNERABILITIES

Human exposure and proneness to manipulations, otherwise called social engineering, accounted for a significant proportion of cyberattack incidents during the pandemic. Just as computers have vulnerabilities, humans also exhibit weaknesses that could expose them to confidence tricks and make them susceptible to psychological manipulations, which can threaten the confidentiality, integrity, or availability of their digital activities in the cyberspace.

4.2.1 Human Factor of Security

In nearly all Cybersecurity incidents that occurred during the pandemic, the human factor was generally utilized by cyber criminals and internet fraudsters as the first step to gain initial unauthorized access to the target's resources and subsequently, launch other exploits to obtain sensitive personal information, manipulate corporate data, and eventually, take full control of the compromised system.

The massive Twitter hack incident of 15th July, 2020 exploited the human factor of security in key employees that possess super user access to critical system functions. That initial entry point availed the hackers the command and control [5] privileges with which they escalated their access levels and launched the massive ransomware attack. The attack compromised the accounts of 130 high profile Twitter users, including Joe Biden and Barack Obama, during which crypto scam tweets were simultaneously sent to millions of the victims' followers. The Twitter incident is discussed in detail under Section 4.4.6.

COVID-19 saw the heightening of the human factor phenomenon largely because of people's desperation to obtain information on the disease, including how to stay safe. People also wanted to transact work and business remotely, learn COVID-19 survival strategies, have access to Government lockdown support funds, and identify from where to purchase cheap masks. In addition, neighbourhoods wanted news updates on drug development, availability of personal protective equipment (PPE), and information on vaccine trials.

These expectations were coming in quick succession amidst the limitations imposed by social distancing restrictions, which compelled the adoption of online alternatives that could not meet security benchmarks, thereby increasing the risks of exploitation of the human factor in cybercrimes.

Some gimmicks even focused on persuading large online groups, blogs, and forums to patronize fictitious COVID-19 information portals for a fee, while displaying fabricated stories of seemingly successful users of such fake portals. The gimmicks were enormous, and all of them targeted human vulnerabilities and shortcomings.

As cyber criminals cashed in on human desperation to deceive internet users and distribute harmful software [3], it became clear that such human vulnerabilities were premised on the fact that every available resource on the novel coronavirus disease provoked attention, appeared attractive, and particularly appealed to the curiosity of the internet users. It was the curiosity of users that further increased their risks of downloading adware, spyware, ransomware, and other malicious software, rather inadvertently or ignorantly. All the cyberattacks that hinged on social engineering during the COVID-19 pandemic were linked to emotional attacks that capitalized on natural human instincts and shortcomings. Various threat actors saw the pandemic as a golden opportunity to capitalize on fear, spread misinformation, and generate mass hysteria [6, 7].

Although detailed discussion on the threats associated with human vulnerabilities is done under the Social Engineering section, the explanations of how inherent weaknesses exposed humans to social engineering cyberattacks during the COVID-19 pandemic have been offered in the following headings, providing an understanding of how the despair and apprehension exhibited by people in the face of seeking for coronavirus interventions also made humans easy targets of cybercrime [2], most of which were cleverly executed to extract valuable and often sensitive information for immediate commercial gains, or later malicious benefits.

4.2.2 Sympathy and Compassion

Out of human kindness, people instinctively exhibited compassion and eagerness to help those purportedly suffering from lack, hunger, isolation, or any form of discomfort due to COVID-19 restrictions.

In the process, internet fraudsters, using deception and pretext, tricked many people into clicking on fake online links, which installed destructive malware that stole their private and confidential data, and in some cases, crashed their personal systems or disrupted smooth operations within organizations. All cases resulted in unintentional or inadvertent breaches. The compromise of 230,000 records of COVID-19 test takers in the electronic database of the Indonesian Government in May 2020 [8, 9] was allegedly orchestrated through social engineering techniques that used compassionate connotation to attract the sympathy of the database operators.

4.2.3 Urgency and Persuasion

By creating the false impression that a fabricated incident required top priority, unsuspecting individual victims or corporate employees were deceived into providing swift action often by clicking on a button to accept a fictitious offer or to download a dangerous file that installed malware capable of compromising sensitive information. This echoed Eric Cole's 2015 assertion that 60% of the cyberattacks in that year were committed by the employees acting either maliciously or inadvertently. During the pandemic, however, the figure rose to about 88% in the healthcare sector owing to the quantum of valuable medical records and patient information being processed.

4.2.4 Desperation and Confusion

The uncertainty and hopelessness that characterized COVID-19 triggered so much despair, anguish, and agony to the extent that some people became frantic in their efforts to seek for helpful information from strange and unfamiliar sources, including clicking on any online content that purported to relate to coronavirus [2].

Such desperate habits of people that arose out of confusion increased the chances of innocently downloading harmful codes, which ended up spying on and stealing their private or sensitive data.

4.2.5 Loyalty, Honesty, and Respect

To portray devotion and faithfulness, victims became vulnerable to accepting, rather ignorantly, any email or online content that purported to originate from familiar superiors, colleagues, family members, constituted authorities, or professional, religious, and political affiliations asking for immediate action.

Responding to such immediate actions as an honest show of respect and solidarity, by clicking on malicious links, was all that the cyberattacker required to install destructive malware on the victim's system to compromise sensitive data. This category of social engineering technique was used to obtain the initial information from external users, which aided hackers in the hijack of two websites [10] belonging to San Francisco International Airport (SFO) in the US in March 2020.

4.2.6 Anger and Grief

Getting infected with the coronavirus disease or losing loved ones was bad enough to cause grief and desolation. However, cyber criminals capitalized on the grief and misery surrounding the disease to entice victims with fake online services and products masqueraded as providing succor, hope, and comfort to those infected or affected in one way or the other.

4.2.7 Fear, Worry, and Anxiety

Both the panic ignited by the COVID-19 pandemic and the distress generated by the disease itself triggered tremendous levels of anxiety that led unsuspecting victims to cling to any available online resources that claimed to provide solutions to their fear and anxiety by offering some form of COVID-19 related support in healthcare, medical advice, palliative grants, protective equipment, and safety tips.

In the process of identifying with those deceptive support services out of sheer anxiety, many internet users fell victims of online scams that compromised the confidentiality of their sensitive information, the integrity of private data, and the availability of their online systems.

4.3 TECHNICAL AND OPERATIONAL VULNERABILITIES

4.3.1 Expired Security Systems

The topmost technical vulnerability that attackers looked out for to aid their exploits during the crisis was the application running expired version of security system. The attackers would easily identify such applications during pre-attack reconnaissance. According to Martin Lockheed's cyber kill chain [11, 12], reconnaissance is an indispensable step of every cyberattack during which the attacker inspects the underlying system parameters to detect vulnerable points on the target system and takes time to plan how best to exploit them and possibly evade detection.

An expired security system poses a challenge to its functionalities and a risk to the networks within which it operates. Security systems having un-renewed licenses are incapable of suppressing newer threats and can expose the entire network to higher risks of attack.

4.3.2 Obsolete Operating Systems (OS) and Utilities

As the livewire of any hardware or software application, the operating systems (OS) requires constant upgrade to keep up with the vendor enhancements, which are largely guided by the user's expectations, technology advancements, and market competition. The continuous use of obsolete and unsupported OS exposes the system to exploits that target weak and poorly protected utilities. A large number of video conferencing breaches during the pandemic was related to systems with either outdated utilities or deficient security features that were incapable of shielding off interception attempts done by the hackers.

- The Zoom application experienced several attacks until the organization addressed key security features that included an improvement on its encryption level to provide increased protection against tampering [13]. Zoom became the App many people used for leisure and work, and to stay in touch with colleagues, friends, and family [14] following the pandemic that forced people to stay indoors and work from home, leaving voice and video calls the only ways of communication. The video conferencing App saw an unprecedented level of growth in the period. However, obsolete security features in the App created a technical vulnerability, which allowed hackers to intrude into conferencing sessions and post obscene footages or disrupt on-going communications, a cyberattack pattern that was tagged as "Zoom-bombing".
- The technical vulnerability which generated several complaints [15–17], including legal actions [18, 19] from the global users, forced the company to review the App, focusing on improving its security and privacy features [13, 20] to allow safer video conferencing sessions.
- A part of the company's strategy to boost the security of the Zoom App was the acquisition of Keybase [21–23], a developer of secure messaging and file-sharing services, to help build scalable

end-to-end encryption into its video-conferencing platform. The optimized App would prevent internet scammers from hacking into teleconferencing calls to interrupt meeting sessions or eavesdropping on confidential communications.

4.3.3 Capacity Gap

As a routine, any deficiency in the technical capacity of in-house workforce to counter cybercrimes poses a challenge for organizations especially those that rely on outsourced services for their operations. Awareness creation on operational ethics for online safety is an essential component of cyberspace protection for both individual and corporate users.

4.3.4 Misplaced Priorities

Prioritization of organizational data classification is usually done based on the value, sensitivity, and worth of such data, matching the same attributes that make them attractive to cyberattacks. Data classification, as a major component of an organization's ICT policy, is expected to provide detailed categorization of corporate data in consideration of its criticality as the key determinant of the level of protection that must be accorded to it.

Naturally, sensitive data needs stronger protection than open data of public knowledge. Critical data routinely requires secure protection to avoid leakage and unauthorized alteration, both of which could lead to stigmatization, reputational damage, and scandal. Apart from the requirements of public disclosure or law enforcement mandates, leakage of confidential corporate trade secrets or of customers' financial information could snowball into crippling litigations, which could potentially challenge the survival of the organization.

The trend of COVID-19 cyberattacks majorly targeted organizations with a reactionary approach to Cybersecurity. Unfortunately, the nature of such cyberattacks was swift, denying such organizations any second chance to prioritize aspects of their business that relied on effective data security. The lack of deliberate ranking of corporate data in order of importance and value was the vulnerable link that exposed them to several threats during the pandemic.

4.3.5 Disrupted Procedures

The devastation caused by the pandemic, especially at the point of lockdown, disrupted the smooth flow of operations in the corporate world across virtually all business sectors ranging from healthcare and hospitality to aviation and pharmaceuticals. The business disruption occasioned by restrictions in movement turned out to be a big operational vulnerability that fueled more cyberattacks.

In some developing countries where electric power supply was either rationed or completely cut in specific localities as personnel worked from home, the disruption led to poor surveillance and a degraded physical security over the ICT infrastructure. The reality of power cuts escalated the vulnerability in such areas and gave rise to cyberattacks, most of which were immediately undetectable and subsequently untraceable, particularly vandalization of data transmission equipment, and burglary of data centre infrastructure.

4.3.6 Administrative Loopholes

The pandemic came with minimal warning, throwing up unprecedented challenges across all sectors. Corporate organizations had no time to make last minute plans to protect their data and digital assets with additional security defense systems. Lack of organizational digital policies and ignorance on the part of individuals also compounded their vulnerability and increased their exposures.

4.3.7 Network and Connectivity Exposures

Although the security of connectivity solutions is non-negotiable, most companies are known to operate with unprotected data in addition to poor network security practices, making them vulnerable to data loss [24]. Connectivity solutions are essential for the efficient exchange of data across diverse computer networks.

However, connectivity-related vulnerabilities accounted for the high success rate of several breaches that were targeted against remote work applications such as the zoom security flaws discussed in Section 4.3.2.

4.4 CYBER THREATS AND EXPLOITS

4.4.1 Cyber Threats

Usually, whoever or whatever attempts to undermine [2] a system or digital service for malicious intent is regarded as a potential threat. The cybercrime domain in the COVID-19 pandemic was largely characterized by organized criminal cyber threats.

Operationally, every cyber threat capitalizes on the presence of a system weakness or human vulnerability to launch a cyberattack to gain a financial advantage, obtain ransom, carry out espionage, inflict online harassment, propagate an ideology, express grief, or deploy mischief.

COVID-19 incidents clearly showed that Cybersecurity threats are evolving at a rapid pace and are increasingly becoming highly sophisticated [25], often with appearances that tend to evade traditional detection techniques [4] and make them to gain persistence in the system [26].

4.4.2 Perspective of the Digital Threat [27]

In a single 24-hour period from 14th April to 15th April, 2020:

- 170,387 spam emails were found to contain "corona" or "COVID" in the subject line.
- 19,694 unique IP addresses were used to send those emails.
- 8,391 unique email domains were used to send those emails.
- 583 of those emails were found to contain an infected attachment, which if clicked, could give the attacker full control of the victim's computer.

This was merely a single day statistic focused on a single type of threat – spam email – monitored under a single threat detection methodology. This gives an idea of the cumulative global impact of many types of threats across multiple systems over the period of months that the pandemic lasted.

4.4.3 Threats to Healthcare Data

As the world's healthcare institutions and medical systems were being stretched to their limits while the pandemic raged in the most affected regions, the need for speedy access to medical data desperately grew owing to the rising cases of new infections [28].

- Frontline medical workers needed credible data to plan for the use of limited facilities.
- Contact tracers needed accurate and timely statistics to support tracking.
- Isolation centres needed demographic data updated in real-time [29] to reflect the changing dynamics of the spread of the virus in order to plan for staffing, supplies, distribution of PPE, and other logistics.

- Hospitals needed health data to manage medications, disease mapping, and hospitalization.
- Pharmaceutical companies required data to plan market segmentation.
- Research institutes needed health statistical records to strategize on clinical analysis of vaccine trials.

In view of the importance of health data in the pandemic and beyond, there was an emphasis on accuracy and speed of generation to justify the high demand, bringing Cybersecurity [3] to the front burner.

4.4.4 Cyber Exploits

Sadly, amid the COVID-19 crisis, malware authors and social engineers were busy exploiting the urgency of the situation for their own personal gain as the cyber threats were never in short supply.

Cyber criminals leveraged the global crisis to launch coordinated cyberattacks on porous networks, particularly targeting systems harbouring unmitigated vulnerabilities. Their activities and cyber exploits denied the much-needed speedy access to health records, medical data, clinical information, and laboratory data required by frontline medics, caregivers, and emergency personnel to respond to the health demands of the moment. This compounded the predicament ever further.

Similar attacks were also targeted against the computing assets and digital infrastructure of logistic organizations, and health funders involved in moving medical supplies across the areas of need. In most of the incidents, the threats were so sophisticated as though hackers were indeed reaping the rewards of groundwork they had laid down and rehearsed several months before COVID-19 struck [30].

The most dominant malware and threats used by hackers during the pandemic were ransomware, virus, social engineering exploits, adware, worm, Trojan horse, logic bomb, spear phishing, man-in-the-middle attack, cyber espionage, and cyber bullying.

4.4.5 Malware

A malicious software (malware) is any hostile software that is deliberately disruptive by design and destructive in operation. The malware author's sole intent is to cause harm and undesirable outcome to its target system. The moment a malware penetrates its victim, it performs disruptive actions, including unauthorized alteration and destruction of data, both of which could restrict the availability of data significantly. Exposition of sensitive data resulting from malware action remains the bane of privacy infringements. A malware could also cause an unpredictable computer malfunction.

The majority of malware incidents that occurred during the COVID-19 pandemic were distributed via the email phishing technique to unsuspecting victims, who simply clicked a harmless-looking internet link (or uniform resource locator – URL) embedded in an email message. Other victims downloaded an infected file which injected the malware payload unto their vulnerable systems. An undetected malware is a serious threat to an unprotected system, as it could become a perpetual source of cyber espionage, stealing, and for exporting confidential data from the victim's computer to a remote collaborating malicious hacker.

There are many types of malware that fall under the category of discussion, and by which internet scammers exploited the pandemic situation to infect unsafe and poorly-protected systems. Table 4.2 captures popular malware threats alongside their operational descriptions.

4.4.6 Ransomware

A ransomware is a malware that prevents its victim from accessing the infected system or file, by blocking login functions and encrypting [31] the victim's critical data, respectively [32], while demanding a ransom [33] within a very tight deadline. Ransomware targets both corporate and residential users [34], and is usually embedded in an email attachment or a clickable download link, which secretly installs the malware payload in the background of the unsuspecting victim's porous system. It is classified as a sophisticated attack vector with many variations and families [11].

Although COVID-19 witnessed a concentration of many of the reported cases of ransomware among IT, e-commerce, and high-tech companies, incidents included coordinated attacks that were targeted at the computing infrastructure of four parallel markets and industries.

Cybersecurity mattered more than ever during COVID-19, and the risk of ransomware increased as a result of the shift to remote working [35], as well as the need for prompt and accurate medical data by frontline health workers and other healthcare personnel.

In general, a ransomware infection is characterized by inability of the victim to login to the system or open files containing critical data

TABLE 4.2 Popular malware threats that dominated COVID-19 pandemic

SN	CATEGORY	SPECIFIC	TARGET INDUSTRIES	IMPACT
1.	Ransomware	• CryptoLocker • CryptoMix Clop • Cyborg • Ekans • Maze • REvil • Robbinhood • Snake encryptor [1] • ThiefQuest [2] • WastedLocker	• Healthcare institutions • Hi-tech & Online • Entertainment • Manufacturing • Real estate • Financial institutions • Education	• Data leak • Data alteration • Data loss • Privacy infringement • System crash • Identity theft • Reputational damage • Revenue loss • Service disruption • Operational inefficiency • Regulatory fines • Forced public disclosure • Stigmatization • Patient trauma • Cyber harassment • Espionage, cyber spying • Email harvest • Denial of service • Litigation • Scandal • Fatality
2.	Other malware (virus, worm Trojan horse, adware and logic bomb, etc.)	• PlugX, Crimson Rat • NanocoreRAT • Zeus Sphinx Trojan [3] • Grandoreiro • EventBot • Trojan-Spy • Cerberus Trojan [4] [5]		•

Source:

[1] Bradley Barth, "No Reprieve for Health Care Orgs as Ransomware Hits Hospital Operator, Plastic Surgeons," SC Media, 6 May 2020. [Online]. Available: https://www. scmagazine.com/home/security-news/ransomware/no-reprieve-for-health-care-orgs-as-ransomware-hits-hospital-operator-plastic-surgeons/ [Accessed 30 July 2020].

[2] Security Lab, "Clop, Clop! It's a TA505 HTML Malspam Analysis," Hornet Security, 7 July 2020. [Online]. Available: https://www.hornetsecurity.com/en/security-information/clop-clop-ta505-html-malspam-analysis/#:~:text=the%20Clop%20ransomware.-,Clop%20ransomware,stage%20of%20an%20TA505%20attack [Accessed 28 July 2020].

[3] Akshaya Asokan, "Enhanced Zeus Sphinx Trojan Used in COVID-19 Schemes," Bank Info Security, 12 May 2020. [Online]. Available: https://www.bankinfosecurity.com/enhanced-zeus-sphinx-trojan-used-in-covid-19-schemes-a-14267 [Accessed 2 August 2020].

[4] Financial Express Online, "Beware of Potentially Dangerous Banking Trojan 'Cerberus' Exploiting COVID-19 Crisis: *CBI,*" *Financial Express, 19 May 2020. [Online]. Available: https://www.financialexpress.com/industry/technology/beware-of-potentially-dangerous-banking-trojan-cerberus-exploiting-covid-19-crisis-cbi/1964269/ [Accessed 2 August 2020].*

[5] Arvind Gunasekar, "Cyber Virus Stealing Credit Card Details Using COVID-19 Information: *CBI,*" *NDTV, 19 May 2020. [Online]. Available: https://www.ndtv.com/india-news/cerberus-coronavirus-malicious-software-stealing-financial-data-using-covid-information-cbi-2231652 [Accessed 19 August 2020].*

which the attacker considers to be of significant commercial value, such as healthcare data. Failed login attempts would usually be accompanied by a hostile message announcing the system as hijacked and files as encrypted. Ransomware extorts users by locking access to computer resources and asking for a monetary payment to recover such access [34]. The hijack message also issues instructions on actions required of the victim to make payment within a very tight deadline [33], obtain the decryption key, and regain access to the system and file.

In most cases, ransomware leaves the user with very few options, such as only allowing the victim to communicate with the attacker to pay the ransom [33]. The samples of typical hijack messages on infected systems by WannaCry [33], Cerber [36], and Bad Rabbit [37, 38] ransomware are shown in Figures 4.1, 4.2, and 4.3.

Unfortunately, in almost all ransomware cases, ransom payment does not necessarily guarantee instant release of encrypted files [39] by the attacker neither does release of decrypted files assure that malware has been totally removed from the infected system [32]. In fact, paying the ransom does not even guarantee that the users will get the decryption key or any unlock tool required to regain access to the infected system or hostage files [40].

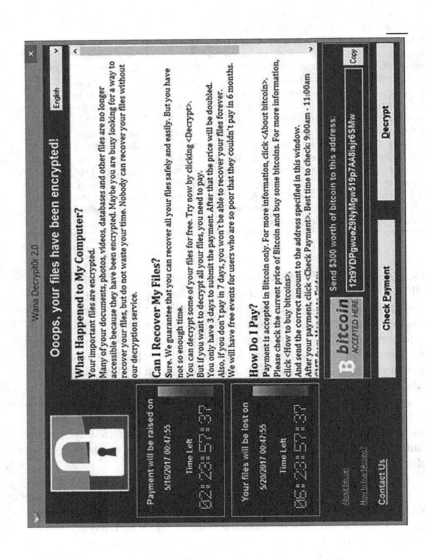

FIGURE 4.1   WannaCry ransomware extortion message.

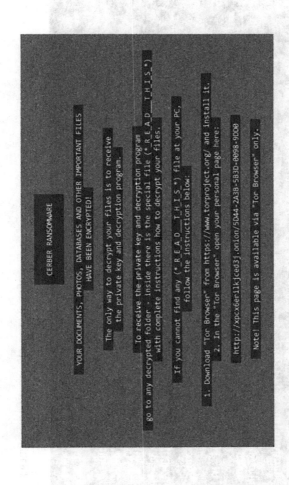

FIGURE 4.2   Cerber ransomware extortion message.

Oops! Your files have been encrypted.

If you see this text, your files are no longer accessible.
You might have been looking for a way to recover your files.
Don't waste your time. No one will be able to recover them without our
decryption service.

We guarantee that you can recover all your files safely. All you
need to do is submit the payment and get the decryption password.

Visit our web service at caforssztxqzf2nm.onion

Your personal installation key#1:

ZMCOKDgX7oKoxrakfBMXAloe8t6McW7Wfx5I+rjJD8hzo6DPpYhNQNCiUjA6GX3w
y4wZX6UdirzbsD7sleuKEndRReez+FLaoEIfQxGsGQ2qUOC4Aaxd7KS8T3O1cOig
Mc1AvUy+r71X6QcIBZe3iI7gqWTbIAqXqUK94dANmsI7hQcrC16q2WwxRjH4rF7e
3sFVVaJW+iWUbY9M+LjnoMqb5zUJzU3yZsj7UCoj4bWTrM093a9pGwyh858vPY21
2LqEcudkJQFSjUmb8FN7E8pSyoZOF4jZ5RRQMSESNRt6hBBxU8o3Geb1SKBEjWIY
giRdOdaIP5unWM8IJA5GkfccbgTVX77Kjg==

If you have already got the password, please enter it below.
Password#1: _

FIGURE 4.3   Bad Rabbit ransomware extortion message.

Ransomware appeared to be the main money-making scheme for cyber criminals [33] and the key threat to the internet users during the pandemic. Although COVID-19 witnessed a concentration of many of the reported cases of ransomware among IT, e-commerce, and high-tech companies, incidents included coordinated attacks targeted at the computing infrastructure of four parallel markets and industries within the healthcare ecosystem, namely:

- Medical facilities.
- Healthcare and pharmaceutical manufacturing companies.
- Medical logistics and transportation organizations.
- Health funding and insurance institutions.

Derived from these listed markets, there are some expanded categories that were worst hit by ransomware and malware threats.

- Hospitals.
- Medical research.
- Medical marketing.
- Pharmaceutical industries.
- Medical supplies.
- Health maintenance organizations.
- Medical laboratories.
- Health insurance organizations.
- Medical manufacturing companies.
- Health education institutes.
- Private health regulators.
- Government health regulators.
- Health funders.

Following the trend of security breaches particularly ransomware, it appeared as though the targets were strategically chosen to reflect the attackers' perception that all four markets possessed critical data that had significant ransom value based on their direct relevance in tackling any of the critical parts of COVID-19 intervention. For example, the digital assets of healthcare institutions, isolation centres, and medical laboratories were targeted because these organizations had operational access to huge data on disease mapping, contact tracing information, and test result respectively, all of which were critical data required for case management, hospitalization control, and trend analysis of infection rate.

On the other hand, the digital assets of pharmaceutical manufacturers and transporters were the targets of ransomware because they were equally believed to possess critical data on drug allergies, trade secrets for vaccine development, and logistic data on the distribution of test kits and PPEs.

The attraction of hackers to IT, e-commerce, and high-tech companies was fueled by the strategic relevance of IT services in providing technology support for the healthcare institutions, which were at the frontline of medical interventions. These companies were also at the epicentre of most ransomware targets due to the value of data held, managed, transacted, or secured by them on behalf of the four parallel markets and industries within the healthcare ecosystem, mentioned earlier.

- On 19th March, 2020, Chinese microblogging company, Sina Weibo, suffered a ransomware attack in which the hackers allegedly stole 538 million user records and offered them for sale on the dark web [41], an incident the company initially denied. The incident prompted regulatory outcries amid reactions over the state of the company's Cybersecurity posture. The leaked user data was mainly personally identifiable information (PII), including phone numbers, locations, count of followers, gender, and passwords.

Sina Weibo, the Chinese equivalent of Twitter [42, 43], is one of the biggest social networking platforms in China, with over 445 million monthly active users as of Q3 2018. Since its launch in August 2009, its popular services have progressively displaced television and newspapers as the country's most important source of information in real-time [44].

In swift response to the security breach, the company updated its interface security strategy, reported details of the incident to law enforcement [45], and shared several mitigation advisories with its users. In March 2012, the Chinese Government had introduced new rules for tracking cybercrimes across the web [44], including mandating users to register on Chinese social networking sites only with their real names, and not with pseudonyms. Real identities were perhaps what made Weibo's user base quite attractive to the hackers, as they represented the owners' actual PII attributes.

The hack which impacted Sina Weibo's reputation also caused a trust deficit among its users.

- On 20th April, 2020, the Indian branch of the American digital and IT services company, Cognizant, was hit by the maze ransomware [4], which affected the employees' personal information as well as the information of the customers' active credit cards – an attack the firm estimated could have potentially imposed up to $70 million cost impact [46]. As the attack caused service disruptions for some clients, Cognizant swiftly made provisions for communication of indicators of compromise (IoC) and other technical information to its customers as an initial mitigation control while perfecting a long-term set of containment, eradication, and recovery measures.

In addition to compromising a number of personal data of associates before the ransomware attack was finally contained on 1st May, 2020 [47], the impact of the cyber breach on Cognizant included the leakage of sensitive internal documents to the public. It also attracted government fines for the PII that got exposed in the process [48].

• On 1st May, 2020, the computer systems of two US-based plastic surgery facilities, Washington-based Bellevue and Tennessee-based Plastic Surgery Center of Nashville, were attacked by a cyber criminal group using the Maze ransomware [49, 50], an attack that purportedly led to patients' sensitive information being posted online. The cyber criminal group reportedly published several large files containing protected health information (PHI) stolen from two separate plastic surgeons for sale on the dark web [51]. The compromised sensitive data exposed by the hackers included patient's full names, dates of birth, social security numbers, appointment details, contact information, as well as medical information on diagnostic codes, histories, and allergies. Vulnerabilities exploited by the Maze ransomware included easy-to-crack passwords and unpatched remote access systems.

The dual attacks on the hospitals repudiated an earlier purported commitment by some cyber gangs to show mercy and abstain from attacking and extorting medical and healthcare providers during the COVID-19 pandemic [50, 52], an action that clearly demonstrates that the adversary has no morals and no ethics [53] and can never be trusted.

• On 6th May, 2020, Germany-based Fresenius, Europe's largest private hospital operator was hit by the malicious Snake encryptor ransomware [50, 54], an attack that threatened its global operations, including dialysis services and medical devices for the care of COVID-19 patients, some of which were being managed for kidney failure. In a swift incident response, the hospital management reported the cybercrime to the relevant investigating authorities [55], while the IT security team isolated key IT systems to prevent further spread after identifying that the vulnerability that led to the attack was most likely linked to social engineering campaign as an entry technique prior to the installation of the ransomware payload.

• On 23rd July, 2020, Garmin – the American GPS, technology and fitness-tracker multinational company was hit by the WastedLocker ransomware attack [56, 57]. The attackers encrypted some of Garmin's vital computer systems and then reportedly demanded US$10 million ransom to restore access [58, 59] in a typical ransomware-as-a-service (RaaS) campaign.

Garmin delivers innovative GPS technology solutions across diverse markets, including aviation, marine, fitness, outdoor recreation, tracking, and mobile apps [60]. The company provides home consumer wearables, sportswear, smartwatches, mapping, and tracking solutions for maritime and automotive industries and owns as much as 46 subsidiaries worldwide with diversified interests in avionics, haulage, manufacturing, navigation system, etc. The WastedLocker ransomware grounded operations across the company's diverse markets of interest.

The action of WastedLocker prevented customers from accessing their connected services [61], including the Garmin Connect, flyGarmin's website and mobile app [62–64], Strava, and inReach solutions. This resulted in the interruption of many of its online services, including map software updates, website functions, customer support, customer facing applications, and company communications.

Although the company did not attribute the breach to Evil Corp., nor mentioned the WastedLocker ransomware [65], the notorious malware was long speculated to be operated by a Russian cybercrime group Evil Corp. [66, 67] allegedly targeting workers trapped at home due to COVID-19 lockdown measured [68].

After days of unbearable downtime and crippled business, Garmin's IT department created an executable file that decrypted a workstation [61] and then installed a variety of security software on the machine, from where gradual restoration [69, 70] commenced to return services to normalcy [71]. Throughout the period of business disruption, Garmin constantly kept millions of its online users updated on status via a conspicuous notice on the index page of its website.

The motivation for the Garmin attack was a fallout of the COVID-19 crisis based on the attractive potentials of huge data which consumers of the company's products and services could have been generating while in lockdown or working from home. This reveals a scary projection for consumers that completely rely on accessing their personal information from online repositories in the custody of third parties.

Although there was no confirmed indication from Garmin that customers' personal information or location was accessed [72], the attack sounded like a wakeup [73] call that the personal data of clients might potentially be at a great risk of devastating leakage in attacks of similar dimension, an example being the Twitter hack of 15th July, 2020.

The Garmin attack further revealed a shift in the pattern of COVID-19 related cyberattacks which found large organizations more profitable to attack, especially those with business interests in leisure, healthcare, manufacturing, and public utilities.

Even as Sina Weibo, Cognizant, Bellevue, Fresenius, Garmin, and other victim organizations recounted their losses and worked hard to regain customer trust and public confidence, there were several other incidents of ransomware that took advantage of loopholes amplified by COVID-19 panic response, or cyberspace vulnerabilities created by the pandemic's uncertainties, including the Twitter breach of 15th July, 2020, which combined social engineering and phishing.

The notorious Clop CryptoMix ransomware equally took advantage of COVID-19 to infect porous Microsoft Windows-based applications. The peculiarity of Clop's operation after infecting a PC lies in the leakage of sensitive information if the negotiation deal for ransom fails. In addition, its payload is constantly updated to avoid detection, indicating that an organized criminal group is behind the ransomware [74], with an ability to install additional password-stealing Trojans.

All ransomware cases analyzed above had one commonality – each case almost certainly led to business disruption, suspicion, corporate reputational damage [4], leakage of customer data, and loss of confidential information. The impacts of a successful ransomware attack are usually more devastating than just the cost of the ransom [75], as organizations can suffer lost productivity, loss of business, inconvenience to customers, and potentially, the permanent loss of data. Therefore, organizations must ensure their security systems and cyber defense protocols are up to date and well set up and also ensure that colleagues working remotely or from home are extra vigilant to recognize and avoid social engineering traps.

4.4.7 Computer Virus

A computer virus (or simply virus) is a malware that negatively alters the structure or composition of other computer programs in the affected system, and in the process, inserts its own destructive code into the new host. A virus is typically triggered by the new vulnerable host due to poor defense or inadequate protective mechanisms. During the COVID-19 crisis, it was obvious that the attention of most cyberspace users was focused on news on disease treatment, cure, vaccine, and spread, to the extent that every online resource that purported to be related to the pandemic was attractive and almost always embraced as genuine and resourceful. The desperation and global panic paved the way for malicious hackers to package computer viruses disguised as resourceful COVID-19 updates and target porous systems and networks.

Capitalizing on this vulnerability window, scammers propagated computer viruses using internet URL links, deceptive websites, SMS messages, internet downloads, and fictitious attachments embedded in unsolicited email messages. Naturally, vulnerable users fell prey and got their systems compromised as soon as the virus payload found its way into the OS of the affected device. The consequences which varied from virus to virus ranged from passive theft of confidential data to active modification of critical system files. While some caused minor impacts such as system slowness and momentary disruption of vital computing functions, others inflicted major and irreversible consequences resulting in permanent system malfunctioning, degraded functionalities, inaccessibility, or total system crash.

- On 8th June, 2020, the data network of the Japanese car maker, Honda, was hit by a massive computer virus attack [76, 77] suspected to have been a SCADA-specific computer virus that typically targets industrial control systems, although having a seeming profile of either the Ekans ransomware [78] or the Snake [79] file encrypting malware.

  The virus momentarily affected Honda's ability to access its computer servers, use email and internal systems as well as transact online with external business associates. Although there was no evidence of loss of PII data [80], the company's production line was impacted leading to the shutdown of its UK plant and the suspension of other operations in North America, Turkey, Italy, and Japan [81] as well as in India and Brazil [77]. The temporary shutdown was to enable adequate containment of the virus, as it did during the 2017 WannaCry ransomware attack [82–84].

  The attack appeared to have been carried out using a hostile software designed to attack the SCADA control systems [85] for a wide variety of industrial facilities like rail, auto factories, nuclear and power plants, water supply, and environmental control systems.

The incident was later brought under control after a few days and production lines reopened [86, 87], but the fact that Honda put production on hold and sent factory workers home pointed to disruption of its manufacturing systems, an anticipated consequence of a computer breach of such magnitude. Additionally, Honda's ability to apply its institutional memory from its experience of being a 2017 WannaCry ransomware attack victim helped the company to recover faster, indicative of good Cybersecurity response ethics.

4.4.8 Adware and Spyware

An adware (short for advertisement malware) is any malware that camouflages itself as an online commercial advertisement of an unrequested product, service, or concept, while harbouring a destructive code that can cause harm to the system upon infection. A spyware is a malware that secretly gathers information from a digital resource about a person or organization without their knowledge and may send such information to another entity, by taking control over the computer without the owner's consent [88].

Operationally, both adware and spyware rely on disguising as a marketing ad purportedly propagating products and services that appear enticing to the target, particularly on a topical matter that would most certainly appeal to the target's interest.

This technique formed part of the initial infiltration of target systems during the COVID-19 pandemic, which saw several enticing adware catch words and phrases intended to provoke interest and install spyware, including the following pop-up captions:

- Hand sanitizer is in stock! We can ship within 24 hours! [53].
- Online COVID-19 tester with instant result, click to install.
- Cheap COVID-19 medications around your neighbourhood.
- Current WHO updates on vaccine production and coronavirus information.
- Latest video on COVID-19 breakthrough, click to watch.
- Want to stay safe in Wuhan? Then, click here.
- Buy certified masks and enjoy free delivery anywhere within the US.
- Looking for the cheapest flights out of the UK? Click here now.

On insecure websites, adware appeared as pop-ups that repeatedly flashed catch words with an emotional appeal that mirrored the events of the COVID-19 pandemic, hoping to lure unsuspecting victims into clicking for more information. Upon clicking, the adware payload installed the hidden harmful code on the insecure system, infecting it and triggering the spate of destructive effects earlier described in Section 4.4.7. The characteristics exhibited by most adware included:

- Appearance as a deceptive link which redirected its victims to an insecure website or portal where they were asked to fill out a short online form for processing, while supplying full names, phone numbers, email addresses and payment details.
- Self-installation into a victim's system and the triggering of an immediate and almost uncontrollable cycle of system reboot, leading to system instability. The resulting denial of service would make the system unable to perform its regular operations until a security mitigation action is undertaken.

4.4.9 Computer Worm

A computer worm is a self-existing malware code, which spreads on a vulnerable network by scanning and replicating itself throughout the nodes on the network without any need of an external trigger as obtainable in a computer virus. Once a network is worm-infected, replication to all porous parts and components of the compromised network becomes inevitable except if the entire system is shutdown, individual systems isolated, and a thorough security disinfection is carried out using an appropriate malware removal tool. These procedures are required in the right sequence to effectively purge the system of worm infection and guarantee that the malware's codes are not persistent even thereafter.

The COVID-19 pandemic saw the emergence of exploitative worms that took advantage of weak defenses caused by COVID-19 induced lapses to crawl into vulnerable networks and systems causing slowness, denial of service, and many other performance hiccups.

4.4.10 Trojan Horse

Hackers use a Trojan horse [89] to secretly install harmful software in their victim's computer system by presenting a resource that is disguised to initially appear useful, beneficial, normal or desirable [88]. The victim of a Trojan horse malware is misled by its innocent appearance in the form of a clickable

URL link, a downloadable software, or a harmless email attachment with a catchy label enclosed as a stealth weapon of cyberattack.

The name Trojans horse, as now referred to a type of computer security threat, was derived from the narrative on the historic gift of a hollow wooden horse on wheels [90] inside which armed [91] Greek soldiers hid during the 1260 BC – 1180 BC battle of Troy [92]. Troy is in the present-day Hissarlik, an area located on the Northwest coast of Turkey. The Trojans who thought that the gigantic wooden horse was an actual gift from Greece, opened their city wall and received it, unknowingly admitting the Greek army into their territory.

The Greek soldiers later at night came out of hiding from the hollow wooden horse and attacked the sleeping Trojans and conquered Troy under the reign of King Agamemnon. The wooden horse on wheels turned out to be a mere subterfuge used to conceal the original goal of the Greek army, which was to attack and conquer the city of Troy after ten years of fruitless siege.

In Cybersecurity, a Trojan horse, or simply a Trojan is any malware that hides its presence and true nature by initially disguising as something useful or attractive to the computer user, thereby misleading the user of its true harmful intent to execute a malicious code, which can lead to many undesirable effects such as encrypting the user's files [88] or downloading and implementing further malicious functionalities.

Due to the uncertainties and anxieties that characterized the COVID-19 pandemic and the desperate priorities of online consumers and computer users to promptly access useful information on staying safe and remaining free from the disease, hackers used Trojan horses in combination with social engineering and email phishing to deploy their cyberattack payload often housing a harmful code intended to illegally extract sensitive personal data or business information from unsuspecting victims, or activate a ransomware or other destructive codes in the process.

Trojans do not self-replicate, but are spread through unintentional or mistaken downloads by unsuspecting users normally in the form an infected email attachment or by visiting an unsafe website.

Cases of Trojan horse attacks were rampant as cyber criminals used the COVID-19 crisis as a lure. In particular, the Zeus Sphinx Trojan became a notorious tool for stealing banking and financial data [93] due to its command-and-control features and strong persistence in the infected system.

- In April 2020, the Brazilian-dominated [94, 95] Grandoreiro Trojan [96] was reportedly used to attack clients in at least ten Spanish financial institutions. The cyberattackers used emails containing COVID-19 related images, which unsuspecting users were asked to open to access a URL that led to a malicious website.

The malicious website in turn installed Grandoreiro's harmful payload that established remote command and control connection with the attackers through which they escalated their privileges and permissions [96] on the infected system and were able to spy on the victim's internet usage, capture banking transaction logins, and steal financial credentials. The elevated privileges also enabled the hackers to deploy disruptive codes that made their track undetectable by weak intrusion and prevention detection systems.

Since 2016, Grandoreiro has been targeting users in Brazil, Mexico, Spain, and Peru [97] through email spams and fake pop-up windows prompting ignorant users to give away sensitive information. Cybersecurity awareness among users [89] is very essential, as the increase in remote work equally increased the attack surface and the risk of business email compromise (BEC). Additionally, it is essential for individuals and corporate organizations to avoid using endpoint protection tools that are either outdated, unpatched, or poorly configured, as these enable Trojans to strive.

- In March 2020, the Android mobile banking Trojan, EventBot [98, 99] emerged. EventBot abused the Android accessibility feature to obtain access to the device's operating system [100, 101], and steal user information. The malware could automatically update its own code and release new features every few days to adjust to encryption variants on different manufacturers.

  During the COVID-19 lockdown, as many people resorted to using their mobile devices for online shopping and manage their bank accounts, the mobile arena became increasingly profitable for cyber criminals [102], who exploited mobile vulnerabilities to steal user data from financial applications, read user SMS messages, and allow the malware to bypass screen lock credentials [103] and two-factor authentication (2FA).

  Once EventBot infected an Android device, the fake app silently siphoned passwords of banking and cryptocurrency apps and intercepted the 2FA text message codes.

- Other Trojans that dominated COVID-19 cyberattacks were the Cerberus [103, 104] and the Trojan-Spy [105]. While Cerberus contacted smartphone users via SMS requesting to click on a deceptive COVID-19 update link, the Trojan-Spy secretly stole financial data from an infected system. Both were notorious for tricking victims into providing personal information and were capable of capturing 2FA details for launching subsequent attacks.

4.4.11 Logic Bomb

A logic bomb is a malware that remains dormant and inactive on an infected system, and only gets triggered by an event, a circumstance, or a scheduled set of events. By design, a logic bomb is destructive, hostile, and harmful to an infected system, but it remains operationally passive until it is activated when a predefined condition is met such as on a specific date and time, upon deletion of a certain class of files, or in the event of sighting a particular keyword, numerical figure, or storage limit. A logic bomb is as devastating as any other type of malware except that it is only activated by a predefined condition. Logic bombs were never in short supply as the COVID-19 pandemic lasted; the most prominent were embedded to compliment ransomware.

4.4.12 Spear Phishing

Phishing is an email impersonation scam that uses email or other electronic communication platforms to formulate dishonest messages intended to deceive recipients into letting out sensitive information ignorantly or inadvertently.

Spear phishing is a Cybersecurity email threat in which the attacker sends a seemingly personalized but deceptive email message in a cleverly-crafted manner in order to obtain sensitive PII, or confidential data from an unsuspecting target, typically a vulnerable high profile recipient such as an organization's security officer, system administrator, company chief executive, a frontline health worker, a notable leader in society, or someone closely-related to these categories of targets.

It is an advanced form of the simple more generalized phishing threat where a malicious hacker attempts to use a misleading and dishonest email message to fraudulently acquire confidential information from a victim often by impersonating the identity of a known, frequent, or trusted sender. Such attacks take several forms, often combining multiple tactics to create the impression of legitimacy [106], genuineness, and a sense of urgency requiring prompt action from the target.

Spear phishing is more targeted [107] and usually involves the attackers conducting background research on their targets to craft a tailored or personalized email that appears to be from trusted sources. It is an impersonation scam that uses email or other electronic communications to deceive recipients into handing over sensitive information [108]. For example, the "from" field in a spear phishing email might contain fake and deceptive email address, leading the recipient to erroneously believe that the message is from a familiar sender. The number of phishing attempts focused on COVID-19 increased by at least 400% [53].

Many COVID-19 cyberattacks began with a phishing campaign [109] that crafted a tailored and personal email message combined with a social engineering gimmick, which directed unsuspecting victims to download a file or access a URL, both of which acted as the carrier of malware which, when installed, facilitated gross financial fraud [110] among other sinister motives.

During the COVID-19 pandemic, incidents of spear phishing became very rampant with several reported cases that made sensational media headlines, while some caused political and diplomatic ripples by virtue of the profiles of their victims, the reputation of the attacked organizations, and the alleged implicated perpetrators.

- On 6th March, 2020, the Missouri-based BJC Healthcare suffered a phishing attack [111] in which the organization publicly disclosed that sensitive data belonging to a number of patients might have been exposed [54], or potentially compromised [51]. The cyberattack which exploited three vulnerable BJC employees' email accounts [112] indicated that an unauthorized person gained access to the employees' email accounts, during which access to patients' PHI might have occurred, including patients' names, dates of birth, medical records, account numbers, as well as treatment/clinical information such as visit dates, provider names, medications, diagnosis, and/or testing information.

  In some instances, patients' social security numbers and drivers' license numbers were also identified within the compromised accounts. The organization named 14 affiliated hospitals and service organizations whose patients' information were included in the affected email accounts.

  To prevent future occurrence, BJC immediately reinforced Cybersecurity education within staff regarding how to identify and avoid suspicious emails, in addition to deploying security enhancements to its email environment. Besides BJC's public disclosure, it also engaged a leading computer forensic firm to assist with the investigation.

- On 22nd April, 2020, the Australia's state, New South Wales (NSW) Government confirmed falling victim to a phishing attack that put citizen data at risk, in which about 50 email accounts of staff members were reportedly accessed [113]. The Government office engaged forensic specialists [114] after formally alerting the incident to police [115] and law enforcement authorities. Although the internal Cybersecurity team was able to stop the attack and limit the impact on customers and services, the attack raised questions about the state of Cybersecurity and other data protection measures among many government departments.

As part of its incident management approach, the NSW Government office maintained an update section on its official website where it provided monthly relevant unfolding information on the incident including on 28th May, 12th June, and 23rd July, respectively [116]. Importantly, the monthly updates provided technical advisory on the required actions over the existing accounts, password reset, handling of suspicious texts and emails, and precautionary measures over requests for personal information over the internet.

All COVID-19 spear phishing attacks had subject matters centred on topics that were related to coronavirus products or information (e.g., treatment options, vaccine trials, virus spread, quarantine survival techniques, etc.), which were justifiably in high demand at that time, given the panic and uncertainty of the moment.

> *... email scams were tailored to recipients within religious groups, informing them of adjustments in modes of worship in line with the social distancing protocols, and asking the recipients to click on a malicious link to guarantee regular updates.*

Figure 4.4 shows two samples of spear phishing emails intercepted at the time of the COVID-19 crisis, targeting specific victims.

In the first sample shown, an impersonated profile of a known sender was smartly presented to the target recipient in the body of the scam email to make the correspondence appear real, authentic, and immediately believable [3], whereas the email was embedded with a malware which, upon installation by downloading the purported form, was capable of stealing the victim's information. The sense of urgency portrayed in the tone of the email requesting the completion of the form before a specified deadline was a ploy to exploit loyalty, honesty, and respect for sense of urgency, as discussed in Section 4.4.16, which took advantage of human flaws to extract sensitive information for malicious intent.

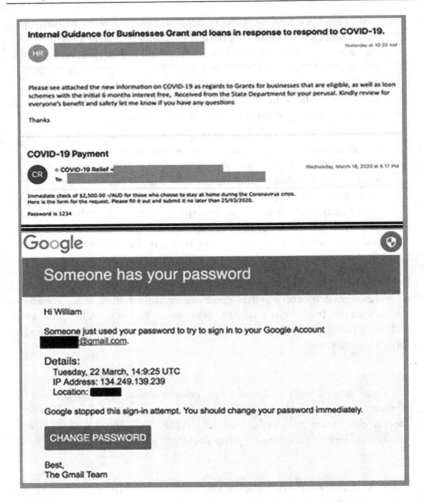

Internal Guidance for Businesses Grant and loans in response to respond to COVID-19.

HR   Yesterday at 10:20 AM

Please see attached the new information on COVID-19 as regards to Grants for businesses that are eligible, as well as loan schemes with the initial 6 months interest free. Received from the State Department for your perusal. Kindly review for everyone's benefit and safety let me know if you have any questions

Thanks

COVID-19 Payment

CR   ◦ COVID-19 Relief <   Wednesday, March 18, 2020 at 6:17 PM
      To:

Immediate check of $2,500.00 √AUD for those who choose to stay at home during the Coronavirus crisis. Here is the form for the request. Please fill it out and submit it no later than 25/03/2020.

Password is 1234

Google

Someone has your password

Hi William

Someone just used your password to try to sign in to your Google Account
██████@gmail.com.

Details:
  Tuesday, 22 March, 14:9:25 UTC
  IP Address: 134.249.139.239
  Location: ████

Google stopped this sign-in attempt. You should change your password immediately.

CHANGE PASSWORD

Best,
The Gmail Team

FIGURE 4.4 Spear phishing samples.

In the second sample, the attacker attempted to create a psychological tension by first notifying the user of his compromised password, and then providing fake timestamps of location, IP address, date, and time of the fictitious compromise in an effort to make the email look real. Finally, the attacker requested the victim to act by clicking on the change password button.

Similar spear phishing emails were received by hospitals and isolation centre managers introducing all kinds of fictitious solutions to them. Some were craftily personalized to face mask production personnel, hand sanitizer distributors, immigration officials, frontline medical personnel, and health insurance agents purportedly offering services related to COVID-19 fight. Some email scams were tailored to recipients within religious groups and faith-based organizations, purportedly informing the congregation of adjustments in modes of worship in line with the social distancing protocols, and asking the recipients to click on a malicious link to guarantee regular updates, a ploy to which ignorant persons fell prey and had their sensitive information compromised.

All phishing emails during the pandemic had a common pattern. They would first attempt to instill fear and a feeling of apprehension by announcing a false critical incident, and then go ahead to request the recipient to take an immediate action to remediate the harm or prevent damage caused by the purported critical incident. Responding to such sense of urgency, out of ignorance, by clicking a button to accept or download completes the attack and infects the system.

Remedies for spear phishing include Cybersecurity awareness, social engineering sensitizations as well as the use of updated operating systems [53], and fully patched applications. It is also essential to install pop-up blockers and end point security tools to detect IoC and prevent eventual compromise. Maintaining a calm disposition in the face of seeming phishing emails while being suspiciously careful is the first step towards conquering the initial distress.

Finally, the use of multiple devices running on separate platforms to check emails and surf the web is an ideal strategy to prevent the unintentional download of malware from a phishing email or at least to minimize its propensity to lead to a total system breakdown.

4.4.13 Man-in-the-Middle Attack

Man-in-the-middle attack, also known as hijack attack, is a Cybersecurity threat in which the attacker secretly intercepts, inserts self in, diverts, alters, or potentially disrupts the real-time communication session between two or more persons or systems that believe they are directly communicating with each other. The motive of man-in-the-middle attack is to harvest personal or corporate confidential information, login credentials, trade secrets, financial information, and other private data for immediate use or later attack.

During the COVID-19 pandemic, the most susceptible services for man-in-the-middle attack were video conferencing, webinar, and remote working sessions. The compulsion to adhere to social distancing protocols and practices meant that a mass workforce working remotely [117] would access network resources and exchange data online with varying degrees of protection, some poor, some strong, and yet some completely inexistent.

The disparity in the security outlook of networks fueled the exponential rise in the incidence of hijack attacks, most of which were only used by the attackers to obtain relevant spy information to launch a bigger attack such as identity fraud, privilege escalation, and ransomware.

Response to the pandemic outbreak led to a surge in teleworking [118], and as employees migrated to their homes to work remotely, cyber criminals equally targeted the vulnerabilities in teleworking systems and networks to gain unauthorized access to corporate organizations across all sectors. One particular technique commonly utilized by cyberattackers was to intercept important data along a communications channel, and make changes to it before sending it on to the intended receiver who is unaware of the alteration, but believes it is from a trusted party. The technique was a major risk to the global efforts to control the spread of COVID-19 as sensitive medical data on disease prevalence faced the threat of circumvention by cybercriminals, who had the disposal of multiple hacking tools to infiltrate porous networks and intercept data transmission with far-reaching impacts.

4.4.14 Cyber Espionage

Cyber espionage is the illegal use of automated tools and computer networks to monitor and trace the digital behaviour or physical mobility of a target, primarily for the purpose of obtaining illicit confidential information without the consent and permission of the target, often for malicious intent or exploitation [119], which potentially impacts national or corporate security, and public safety.

Owing to the restricted mobility imposed by the COVID-19 lockdown measures, and especially the imposition of movement restriction, border closure, and embargo on social gathering, malicious hackers saw an opportunity to spy on their targets using digital tools to track movement trends, monitor online footprints, attempt identity theft, and in some cases, intercept phone conversations and video conferencing sessions, to obtain confidential information pertaining to an individual victim, a government institution, a competitor, a rival group, or a corporate organization.

Throughout the pandemic, especially during and immediately after the massive lockdown, cyber espionage, or malicious reconnaissance, was identified as a prelude to most security breaches, and in most cases, served as an aid to hackers, who relied on its combination with social engineering, for secretly gathering initial intelligence required to launch more coordinated attacks.

- The hijack of two websites owned by SFO Airport in the US in March 2020 started with the hackers spying on the available vulnerabilities that could be exploited. During the covert espionage preceding the exploit, the attackers were able to discover the unpatched security flaws in the Server Message Block (SMB) protocol, a Windows-based protocol for sharing access to files, printers, serial ports, and other resources on the network. Cyber espionage was a tool in their hands with which they identified the weakest component which they eventually capitalized on to facilitate the attack.

- By embarking on a prolonged initial spying on the Indonesian Government's electronic database in May 2020, records of 230,000 people who had undergone COVID-19 testing were allegedly breached [8] in the city of Bali. The cyber criminals used espionage to establish the size and value of the records, which were the attractions that motivated the compromise.

- In the Twitter cyber breach of July 2020 [120], the hackers might probably have obtained all preliminary information through persistent espionage on the company's security architecture for such a long period that they were able to identify vulnerabilities that armed them to attack using social engineering to craftily extract parameters to compromise system login controls, and beat available defense mechanisms.

Cyber espionage is almost always the first stage of a coordinated attack during which cyber criminals gather minute details to aid attack. This threat can be mitigated by subjecting employees to comprehensive Cybersecurity awareness to sensitize them on identifying IoC that might suggest a spying activity. Additionally, an effective anti-spyware and anti-malware tool is essential for automating the detection of suspected espionage activities and alerting relevant personnel promptly. The dangers of retaining outdated utilities can be ameliorated by regular updates, and by maintaining an elaborate security policy.

4.4.15 Cyber Bullying

Cyber bullying is the act of victimizing or harassing a person or group of persons using the internet or other online platforms, including, but not limited to, email, SMS, blogs, online forum, social media, etc. Most incidents of cyber bullying originate anonymously as the attacker conceals his identity to evade recognition. Hiding under the anonymity of the sender, the malicious intent of cyber bullying is to make the victim(s) miserable or psychologically tortured by inflicting emotional or verbal abuse through words, images, video, deep fakes, animation, manipulated sound recording, synthesized voice, or other contents that are insulting, offensive, derogatory, hateful, abusive, threatening, or annoying.

In extreme cases, social media related cyber bullying triggers hate speech, by amplifying conspiracy theories [121] through the posting of obscene contents, indecent images, or extreme skepticism across cultures, religious affiliations, political inclinations, and varying ideologies. Social media has created a world in which any individual can potentially reach as many people as the mainstream media [122], thereby unwittingly promoting anonymous antagonism using the cyberspace as the guerilla battle field, and cyber bullying as the arsenal.

In instances where cyber bullying is not portraying outright falsehood or libel against the victim, it often propagates the seemingly genuine message as a mockery or ridicule, in a sarcastic manner simply to bully and persecute the victim.

COVID-19 pandemic saw a lot of cyber bullying targeted against political leaders and influential institutions through slanderous electronic publications, social media propaganda, and anonymous viral video and audio contents. Violent online criticisms trailed some hasty decisions at the time of lockdown which were initially viewed by certain sections of the public as either exploitative or inhuman. Some of the threats which were propagated via unsolicited chain emails, social media posts, and online tweets came with heavy emotional sensitivities, contempt, and obscenities.

- On 30th May, 2020, following the President Donald Trump's 29th May speech in which he indicated his intention to withdraw US funding of the World Health Organization over alleged WHO's failure in its "basic duty" and purported information mismanagement of the pandemic's early stages in favour of China [123, 124], and formally communicated this to the United Nations to be effective as of 6th July, 2021 [125,126], the global social media went agog with reactionary messages and tweets, containing eulogies [127], satires [128, 129] and criticisms [130–134] alike.

  While some applauded the President Donald Trump's moves describing it as bold, others hid under the anonymity of social media in a typical online harassment fashion to rain abuses and condemnation not only on his person but also on the office of the US President. The malicious trend which was indicative of mass cyber bullying was intended to malign, demonize, and victimize the President while relying on online technologies for speedy propagation, wider spread, concealment, and deeper impact.

- On 1st April, 2020, two days after the President Muhammadu Buhari imposed the initial 14-day lockdown in Nigeria following the discovery of an Italian citizen index case of COVID-19, and as the Nigerian government security agencies were enforcing compliance with the stay-at-home order imposed on some states where the cases were rising at the time, a viral video captioned "brutality of the Nigerian Police" emerged showing a group of defenseless locales allegedly being physically brutalized by uniformed security personnel purportedly attempting to enforce the ban on social gathering.

  Eventually, the viral video turned out to be a doctored clip from a six-year-old event that occurred elsewhere in an entirely different part of Africa where state security was routinely quelling violent rioters using commensurate coercion. That was a classic case of cyber bullying where the online fraudsters capitalized on social media anonymity and created an offensive content, gave it a sensational caption, and pushed it into the cyberspace relying on the fast and wide coverage of online platforms, simply to malign and tannish the integrity, discipline, and professionalism of the Nigerian Police Force (NPF).

- In several blogs and social media platforms, anonymous users posted offensive and indecent cartoons of notable leaders portraying their alleged misconceptions about shortages of medical supplies and ventilators for COVID-19 patients. Some online users fabricated criticisms that over-exaggerated loopholes with contact tracing, inefficiencies with the rapid test kits, and their perceived unequitable distribution of palliative items to local communities worst hit by the virus. There were also computer animations depicting leaders being burnt in effigy as a mockery over their alleged inability to manage hiccups arising from quarantine procedures, and many other alleged inconsistencies.

  The bloggers simply exploited the facelessness of social media identities and the potentials of electronic communications to engage in cyber bullying of their targets by pushing out contents merely intended to harass, victimize, and abuse their victims.

4.4.16 Social Engineering

Social engineering is the dubious art of exploiting human weakness to obtain sensitive or secret information or to gain unauthorized access. Cyber criminals and internet fraudsters utilize this psychological exploitation technique to retrieve sensitive information that can be reused to launch further attack.

Most of the online frauds that took place during the pandemic centred around malicious hackers who were able to manipulate innocent people [135] and employees into performing actions or divulging confidential information out of curiosity to receive purported COVID-19 incentives, or in response to the fear and panic skillfully created by the attacker over the COVID-19 subject. These innocent people are ordinarily harmless and would not cause damage, but they are usually tricked or manipulated into doing something they ordinarily would not do [136].

Throughout the pandemic, scammers used social engineering to skillfully manipulate people and carry out emotional attacks targeting human weaknesses using anxiety, panic, desperation, urgency, fear, loyalty, compassion, confusion, respect, honesty, persuasion, etc. In each case, the anxiety and uncertainty that surrounded the spreading COVID-19, and the curiosity created by the cyberattacker, both led to an unusual clinging to digital systems to know more about the situation, thereby proliferating the incidents of social engineering attack. Social engineers usually employ piggybacking, tailgating, eavesdropping, and shoulder surfing as parts of their deception tools.

Many COVID-19 social engineering and related cyberattacks made sensational headlines owing to the status of victims as well as the political, diplomatic, and business affiliations which they represent.

- On 15th July, 2020, Twitter recorded a massive social engineering attack [108, 120] on some of its employees, which resulted in the compromise of the users' accounts belonging to some famous tech executives, philanthropists, and politicians, including Bill Gates, Barack Obama, Elon Musk, Joe Biden, Michael Bloomberg, and Kanye West. The cyberattackers compromised the targets' accounts by bypassing Twitter's access control and posting self-styled bitcoin messages, shown in Figure 4.5, which turned out to be orchestrated scams. Bitcoin is an electronic payment system [137] that relies on cryptographic proof instead of trust, hence a cryptocurrency.

Although the 15th July social engineering attacks were found to be coordinated scams and the cryptocurrency tweets were not particularly new, the number of affected users was unusually high. The hackers compromised the accounts of 130 high-profile users and were able to reset the passwords of 45 of those accounts [138]. The attack successfully targeted some Twitter employees [139–141] with access to internal systems and tools, through which the scam was orchestrated and launched.

FIGURE 4.5 Screenshots showing hacks on Twitter accounts of Bill Gates and Elon Musk.

The Twitter security breach highlighted an inadequate awareness, a major flaw with a social media service relied upon by millions of people as an essential communications tool, and raised serious reputational and trust issues typical of such high-profile incident. The attackers used phone scams to fool the employees to gain access to the internal systems, after concerted attempts [108] that eventually exploited their human vulnerabilities.

The COVID-19 crisis could have fueled the Twitter attack since the majority of Twitter's employees were either working from home or remotely [140] in compliance with the adjustments in work procedures. It is likely that this could have potentially impacted the security posture of the company since employees with access to sensitive systems and tools found themselves working from remote locations more difficult to protect than working within the corporate network with its fortified security systems.

4.4.16.1 Lessons from the Twitter incident

Two lessons can be drawn: first from Twitter's angle, and then from users' angle.

On the part of Twitter, greater attention to creating staff awareness on social engineering would have minimized the attackers' chances of successfully tricking employees into inadvertently letting out sensitive information. The exposed systems made the bypass of credentials possible for the attackers. With the peculiarity of COVID-19 and the remote work that became pervasive, more sensitization was required to sufficiently arm personnel with the knowledge of new techniques of attack employed by hackers and the actions required to avoid falling prey.

Besides, the defense systems were expected to identify as precisely as the IoC were flagged. At that point, a combination of alerts and automated shutdown of vulnerable systems would have prevented the simultaneous user compromises that resulted in those crypto scam tweets purportedly requesting for Bit Coin (BTC) payments from millions of the victims' followers. Artificial intelligence's predictive analytics and big data are the concepts that will redefine threat hunting in post COVID-19 Cybersecurity.

On the part of Twitter users that fell prey for the BTC scam, their susceptibility to have succumbed to such deception revealed their low level of awareness to the nature and appearance of online threats. Social engineering only succeeds when people do not apply online caution in responding to their human perceptions of urgency, appeal, and sympathy – three human attributes that were exploited in the Twitter attack. Only a five-minute hesitation to challenge why Bill Gates would choose to use a social networking platform for personalized philanthropy would have exposed the deceitful intent of the attackers. Such reluctance was lacking from the users that responded to the BTC tweets with instant payments.

There is a need for more aggressive social engineering awareness. Perhaps, as part of its corporate social responsibility, Twitter could embark on a customized sensitization of each user on how best to identify scam tweets and what actions to take on them. Sending such customized sensitization tweets to each user is possible and could be tailored to mirror user's digital footprint in terms of internet transaction pattern, geographic location, age bracket, online behaviour, and other indices that personalize the mass message.

In general, social engineering has remained a lucrative tool for cyberattackers who are very quick to capitalize on the situational frailties and intrinsic shortcomings in humans to mislead and defraud people. COVID-19 only heightened the susceptibility of people to such gimmicks. Securing people and the information systems on which they depend [142] is an indisputable Cybersecurity goal, and therefore, a suggested remedy is the institutionalization of a culture of aggressive Cybersecurity awareness and social engineering sensitization undertaken on a continuous basis.

4.4.17 Password Abuse

A password is merely one of the many techniques of verifying the identity of a user on a digital system or online resource, a process broadly referred to as authentication. User authentication can be achieved by using either a physical token such as a badge, a unique biometric attribute such as fingerprint, or a memorized secret.

A password is an example of authentication by a memorized secret, as opposed to the authentication by what the user possesses (a token) or by what the user is (biometrics). The global standards and guidelines for password management and complexity specify how to create a strong password by combinations of upper cases, lower cases, special characters, numbers, and their sequencing. Such password and identity management guidelines include specifications by the National Institute of Standards and Technology (NIST) and the SANS Institute [143–145].

Password abuse is the exploitation of a weak or poorly-protected password by an attacker for the purpose of reusing the compromised password for unauthorized access and illicit operations such as identity theft and financial fraud.

Due to the typical proliferation of computing applications and services, users face the challenge of remembering many passwords, each for a different application, to such a count that they become difficult to manage, leading to a phenomenon called password chaos. Remembering a number of passwords can become so complex that the user finds it difficult to memorize accurately, and resorts to unsafe actions to aid memory, including scribbling them on a paper hidden under the keyboard or pasted on the computer monitor. Such insecure actions undertaken to alleviate password chaos that expose the password to easy compromise are collectively known as password fatigue.

In the COVID-19 pandemic, the most prevalent types of password fatigue were the use of weak passwords, and the recycling and sharing of old passwords primarily to avoid the perceived inconveniences of having to remember too many passwords on shared systems. These practices were a major threat which malicious hackers exploited to launch password attacks:

- Dictionary attack to crack weak passwords.
- Brute force to crack stronger but unchanged passwords.

- Social engineering to deceptively obtain other memorized authentication secrets.
- Spear phishing to mislead users into divulging information that could aid any of these techniques.

Since password-related login threats ordinarily account for about 80% of cyber-fraud cases, it is important to evolve solutions that could authenticate users based on who the user is, rather than what the user knows by memory. Biometrics, the use of two-factor authentication (2FA), and single sign-on (SSO) provide secure alternatives to the reliance on mere password for authentication.

During the COVID-19 lockdown, particularly at the point when remote work and social isolation were the watchwords, the combination of biometrics and 2FA provided shield against cyberattacks for organizations that adopted it as their authentication model, and minimized their chances of falling prey to the password abuse incidents. Some pharmaceutical companies and automated isolation centres adopted the model, in addition to medical facilities where ventilators were in heavy use and restricted access was a mandatory safety requirement.

4.4.18 DDoS Attack

A distributed denial of service (DDoS) is a cyberattack in which the attacker deliberately overloads the target system with so much invalid network traffic, e.g. by sending a massive amount of unnecessary messages to a server, to such a point that it overwhelms its capacity to cope with legitimate network traffic, thereby leading to a malfunction, incessant bouts of reboots, or an outright breakdown.

The malicious goal of a DDoS is to disrupt the system's normal operations by making its resources inaccessible and unavailable to the intended users, and in the process, creating an opportunity for the attacker to carry out information theft, data alteration, or installation of harmful code, amid many other possible exploits.

During the COVID-19 pandemic, there were several security breaches that mirrored the profile of the DDoS attacks with negative impacts on system performance. The majority of the DDoS incidents were used at the initial stages of the respective attacks to get critical servers and computing resources busy with excessive unnecessary traffic while the exploit took place undetected.

- On 6th March, 2020, three employees' accounts of BJC, a Missouri-based Healthcare organization, fell victims of the DDoS, which was believed to have initiated a phishing attack using social engineering as an aid. While the DDoS technique flooded the victims' accounts with phishing emails to divert their attention and ignite anxiety, the social engineering component exploited their human vulnerabilities of loyalty to work, compassion for COVID-19 patients, and the sense of urgency conveyed by the tone of the deceptive emails.

The attack resulted in the leakage of PII and PHI, including sensitive medical records, clinical information, as well as treatment data such as patients' names, appointment dates, medication list, lab tests, etc.

The DDoS attacks are typically mitigated using adequate security tools that combine detection with prevention. Intrusion detection and prevention systems (IDS and IPS) automatically watch out for patterns that pose the risk of flooding the network with unnecessary traffic, and either truncate their progression proactively, or alert a human agent for manual intervention.

4.4.19 Fake Website

A fake website also called a cloned website is an illegally-duplicated copy of a legitimately existing website carried out by internet hackers to trick users, spread misinformation, and fraudulently obtain private information from unsuspecting users of the cloned version.

The internet, as it is currently known, is full of websites that are either fake or fraudulent [106], and COVID-19 witnessed the cloning of many prominent websites around the globe for malicious intent, and unfortunately for which many fell victims of not being able to distinguish from the authentic websites due to the dexterity of the hackers and the anxiety that characterized COVID-19.

- In early May 2020, one such cloned website surfaced in Nigeria, with contents that misinformed the public about a fictitious Federal Government approval for the disbursement of funds under a false COVID-19 vote called "Lockdown Funds" [146]. The deceptive website then required the users to complete an online form providing their personal information, including bank details, for the purported payment to be effected.

  Following the discovery, the Nigerian Government's technology regulatory and anti-graft authorities through the National Information Technology Development Agency (NITDA) [147, 148], the Nigerian Communications Commission (NCC) [149–151], and the Economic and Financial Crimes Commission (EFCC) [152] were very prompt in issuing public disclaimers warning citizens to ignore the fictitious website, a proactive move that created so much awareness that people became well-informed of the potential impacts of falling for such gimmicks.

- As part of its roles to ensure a safe and secure Nigerian cyberspace, NITDA's Computer Emergency Readiness and Response Team (CERRT) identified and neutralized a number of websites that were using various phishing tricks to attract internet users in the guise of COVID-19 palliatives or related services, alerting the general public in each case and providing relevant information to maintain online safety.

The pandemic witnessed hackers who launched websites that looked genuine and legitimate but were mere replicas. People who visited such fake websites [153] faced the risk of losing control of their devices in addition to getting misinformed to the extent of incurring financial losses in payments for scam services and decoy products. In extreme cases, victims were tricked into disclosing banking transactions details that facilitated financial fraud.

The remedy for dealing with fake websites are three folds:

- Deployment of adequate Cybersecurity awareness.
- Adherence to cyber ethics and social engineering guidelines.
- Use of multifactor authentication, e.g. 2FA for added protection of financial transactions.

4.4.20 Website Hijack

In a typical website hijack, the attacker hacks into an existing website, takes full control of its maintenance tools, including content management system, and alters its contents to reflect a sinister motive. In some cases, the hacker makes the website inaccessible to its legitimate content managers by encrypting all login paths while demanding for ransom as a condition for release of decryption keys.

The COVID-19 crisis saw the hijack of corporate websites across the globe with its attendant impacts on organizational reputation, client trust, and revenue loss.

- In March 2020, just at the peak of the global lockdown, two websites owned and maintained by SFO Airport, the seventh busiest airport in the US, were hacked, leading to momentary inaccessibility and the leakage of some users' login credentials [10, 154,

155]. The breach compelled the airport to force a reset of all SFO-related email and network passwords even as the originators of the attack were unclear [156].

The known vulnerability was allegedly traced to the external users of Microsoft Internet Explorer web browser who had unpatched security flaws in the Server Message Block (SMB) protocol [157] running on their Windows-based personal devices.

As part of the incident response that followed the data breach, the airport's External Affairs Office issued a public notice [158] advising all persons who had visited either of the two websites using the Microsoft Internet Explorer web browser outside of its managed network, to change their device's password. The airport's public notification was in clear compliance with the global Cybersecurity ethics that requires security events of such magnitude to be reported to the relevant authorities while sharing the lessons learnt with those that were directly affected to sensitize them on what actually happened, what information was involved in the compromise, what actions the organization had taken, and the expectations from users.

Malicious codes were also removed from the affected websites as part of mitigation process to forestall further spread and end the inaccessibility by the legitimate users.

The attack ironically emphasized the security hygiene as an important aspect of maintaining unhindered access to data by the legitimate users of digital resources, including website contents, databases, cloud applications, and online portals.

- On 8th June, 2020, Avon, the UK-based cosmetics giant was forced to shut down its UK website in the wake of a cyberattack [159]. Avon disclosed the breach in a formal notification to the US Securities and Exchange Commission (SEC) on 9th June and a follow-up on 12th June, 2020 [160].
- The breach which potentially exposed 19 million PII records on customers, including full names, phone numbers, dates of birth, email and home addresses, and GPS coordinates [161], as well as internal logs [162] could have potentially attracted the hackers to attempt establishing full server control to conduct severely damaging actions such as ransomware or website hijack. An alleged discovery by safety detectives [163] indicated that Avon might have inadvertently left its Microsoft Azure server exposed to the public internet without password protection or encryption [162], although no link was confirmed between the unsecured server and the breach.

Most website hijacks in the time of the pandemic capitalized on misconfigurations and vulnerabilities in WordPress, the free and open-source web content management system used by over 35% of all websites [164]. About 98% of the WordPress vulnerabilities are currently related to plugins, and the most popular vulnerability types in WordPress plugins are Cross-site Scripting and SQL Injection, both of which refer to the inability of the system to reject external queries crafted and issued through the address field of popular web browsers.

In the most extreme cases such as hacktivism [165, 166], website hijackers typically defaced their victim's homepage with obscene images and a screaming banner with an inscription that announced their mission, and politically-motivated objectives when carried out by a hacktivist group.

4.4.21 Insider Collusion

The sudden and unprecedented transition of countless employees, contractors and third parties to remote work due to the COVID-19 lockdown protocols, left many organizations unprepared to monitor or detect insider threats [119] that may have arisen through deceitful cooperation with other internal or external parties to commit fraud or harm the organization. Cases of employees or ex-employees that initiated, aided, and facilitated cybercrimes were experienced involving internal contacts that deliberately provided intruder access to circumvent systems by capitalizing on a yet-to-be-mitigated vulnerability.

Originally, issues bothering on insider threats [136] whereby employees and individuals acting ignorantly or maliciously to sabotage data resources have been a known phenomenon. Collusion cases normally involve insiders and authorized users with active computer accounts at the time of incident.

- On 16th April, 2020, the US Department of Justice charged a former employee of Stradis Healthcare [167], an Atlanta-based medical device packaging company, for carrying out computer intrusion against his former employer's shipping system, which "allegedly disrupted the delivery of PPE - particularly face masks, gloves and gowns - in the middle of the global pandemic" [168, 169]. The insider attack was allegedly perpetrated barely three days after the former employee received his final termination paycheck [119], obviously disgruntled and frustrated.

  The unhappy former employee deleted approximately 115,581 sensitive shipping records and edited approximately 2,371 others using a previously-created fake account. Although the intrusion was detected on 29th March and reported to the Federal Bureau of Investigation

(FBI) on 7th April, the company was swift to deactivate the fake account, executed some recoveries and contained the insider attack.

On 10th July, 2020, the accused allegedly pleaded guilty to the charge of reckless damage to a protected computer for deleting and modifying his former employer's electronic shipping and other business records [170–172].

- On 4th May, 2020, the San Mateo, California-based online video game company, Roblox, allegedly experienced an insider type cyberattack [119, 173] during which its back end customer support panel was reportedly compromised with the alleged cooperation of an employee, who was reportedly bribed [174, 175] by the hacker. The hacker gained access and could have potentially viewed user account info, reset passwords, granted virtual in-game currency, and removed 2FA from their accounts.

  The company reported the breach to a bug bounty platform, HackerOne, which recognizes and compensates individuals for reporting bugs, especially those pertaining to security exploits and vulnerabilities. However, the hacker had other sinister motives as allegedly portrayed by his tampering of users' passwords and 2FA.

In addition, there were insider threats using telecommuting and work from home sessions where participating employees deliberately released meeting IDs or other credentials to non-members for malicious intent. In some collusion cases, known bugs were intentionally overlooked to the advantage of the intruder and his collaborating internal contacts.

As a mitigation, adequate Cybersecurity awareness is essential, but most importantly, internal controls should include measures to prevent authorization creep where individuals with superior access levels to systems are able to escalate or retain their access even after exiting the organization or switching departments and roles. Other measures include compulsory job rotation, mandatory vacation, need to know, and least privilege.

4.5. CYBERSECURITY IMPACTS OF COVID-19

The potential impacts of cyberattacks on organizations and individuals differ depending on a number of factors [12], including the adversaries' intent, their sophistication and capabilities, their familiarity with automated processes, as well as the nature and porosity of the target resource.

The COVID-19 pandemic and the increased rate of cyberattacks it invoked had wider implications that stretched beyond the immediate targets [110], with many of such implications showing indications of perpetuity. It is the permanency tendency of the impacts of COVID-19 induced cyberattacks that made some of them a major source of concern.

During the pandemic, Cybersecurity breaches arising from various threats and exploits had diverse degrees of impacts on individuals, organizations, governments, groups, and the society. It was evident that the surge in online transactions would open potential avenues for hacking and other malicious cyber events targeting vulnerable systems of commercial value, using phishing emails as the malware propagation tool, and social engineering as the tactics.

4.5.1 Identity Theft

Identity theft and data misuse, including unauthorized disclosure and destruction of data, would ordinarily emerge as impacts of cyber espionage and spear phishing attacks on the exposed corporate information.

As the pandemic raged, and as the adoption of online services became the widely accepted alternative to workspace activities, leisure and business in response to the requirements of the social distancing protocol, it also meant that exposure and risk of theft of inadequately protected confidential data by internet fraudsters would increase. Poorly secured work from home systems were the most vulnerable and most hit telecommuting targets, particularly using the man-in-the-middle attack through the popular zoom-bombing variant.

Incidents of interception of sensitive data being transmitted across unsafe telecommunication channels and poorly protected telecommuting terminals became the fuel for fraudulent bank transactions, unauthorized assess, ransom advantage, and arsenal for future cyber criminalities.

- On 17th April, 2020, 20 million user account details of Aptoide, a third party software "marketplace" App for installing mobile Android applications [176], were leaked on an online hacking forum [177, 178]. The leaked user information, mostly identified as the PII included user's email address, hashed password, real names, sign-up date, sign-up IP address, device details, and date of birth. The identity theft incident also revealed the status of the compromised accounts among many other sensitive technical information.

- On 24th April, 2020, Japanese gaming company, Nintendo, disclosed that hackers illegally gained unauthorized access to 160,000 of its user accounts [179, 180], a figure that later rose by additional 140,000 in June [181]. The hack came amid the COVID-19 pandemic, which led to a surge in Nintendo Switch sales as people sought to entertain themselves with games while quarantined [180].

The hackers compromised the legacy Nintendo Network ID (NNID) login integration system to gain access to Nintendo profiles. The NNID manages accounts on the old Nintendo 3DS gaming platforms. As the hackers gained access to the personal information, including birthdays and email addresses, Nintendo later identified the vulnerability that caused the account hack was the inability of the system to prevent users from maintaining the same password on both their NNID and Nintendo accounts [182]. As an immediate mitigation of the impacts of the cybercrime, the company was compelled to issue a password reset advisory to its users, and apologetically pledged to strengthen security and ensure safety to avoid a repeat of similar event in the future.

Depending on the nature and sensitivity of the stolen corporate data, loss of trade secrets threatened the survivability of affected organizations. For example, in the healthcare sector, loss, or unauthorized modification of patient's medical records exposed patients to the risks of misdiagnosis and mis-prescription, both of which had the long-term tendency to result in fatalities.

During the pandemic, there were far-reaching impacts in many other sectors, affecting operations in government, financial institutions, retail business, e-commerce, and hospitality.

4.5.2 Privacy Issues

Data leaks were rampant during the COVID-19 pandemic owing to the proliferation of cyber breaches on account of poorly protected networks and insecure telecommuting systems that were incapable of preventing, detecting, or proactively responding to the increasing number of cyber threats that characterized the period.

- The Twitter hack of 15th July 2020, for example, was clearly an unprecedented attack on the privacy, trust, and security [183], compounded by poor access control mechanisms amid social engineering vulnerable employees. This combination led to total hijack by the hackers, resulted in an overbearing negative impact on the reputation of the affected users, and raised fears of high-profile litigations.

The number of user accounts compromised in the Twitter incident was a clear indication of privacy infringements, as the hackers compromised 130 accounts, tweeted from 45 of them, had direct access to 36 message inboxes, and downloaded Twitter data from 7.

Ordinarily, litigations triggered by privacy breaches and data protection can go further than mere defamation [184], with civil litigations now shaping important Cybersecurity norms [185]. This raises questions on data ownership and responsibility for liability following a privacy inversion linked to a Cybersecurity breach.

4.5.3 Data Accessibility Issues

The difficulties of accessing data during the COVID-19 pandemic left memorable impacts. It also raised important questions about opening, sharing, and using data [186] for the benefit of containing the spread of the virus, treatment of patients, and making informed decisions.

By their very nature, certain types of cyber threats, particularly ransomware, denial of service, and virus action could be overwhelming in their impacts on digital systems. During the pandemic, this class of threats disabled vital applications, grounded network performance, and led to inoperative networks, which hampered easy accessibility to data for the affected organizations.

The slow or unreachable networks that arose from security breaches represented a nightmare for service organizations that relied on prompt availability of data at the point of need across the COVID-19 response chain. The impact of data inaccessibility could be felt when public health leaders who made the hard decisions had restricted access to high-quality data on key questions [187] such as:

- Where is the disease likely to spread to?
- Does the two-day weather information support flight operations?
- Are there priority areas that we need to contain to limit further propagation?
- How much emergency fund do we require to procure life support systems?
- Where are the most vulnerable communities?

Delayed access to data imposed life-threatening impacts on service organizations that relied on its timeliness for services such as aviation, emergency medical supplies, medical laboratory testing centres, and fitness.

- The March 2020 hijack of two websites belonging to the SFO Airport led to data inaccessibility and ironically emphasized on security hygiene as an important aspect of maintaining unhindered access to data by legitimate users of digital resources, including website contents, databases, cloud applications, and online portals.
- The unauthorized modification and illegal deletion of data by a former employee of Stradis Healthcare [167] in Atlanta's famous insider threat in April 2020, completely denied the company of access to operational data and disrupted its ability to promptly deliver PPE to the areas of need.
- In May 2020, the Indonesian Government's MySQL database containing records of people who had undergone COVID-19 testing was allegedly breached [8] in the city Bali during which approximately 230,000 records were purportedly compromised and their personal data exposed for sale on the dark web's data-exchange platform, Raid Forums.

  Although the Indonesian Government later denied any such incident [188], its National Cyber and Encryption Agency (Badan Siber dan Sandi Negara – BSSN) under the supervision of the Ministry of Communication and Informatics [189] launched an investigation, which required a temporary shutdown of the database during which the test takers could not access their results.

- The ransomware attack on the computers of Garmin, the global technology conglomerate, on 23rd July, 2020 caused a global outage that shut down the company's website, disrupted production lines, and prevented users from uploading their activities. Such large-scale inaccessibility of Garmin's data resources on account of a security breach potentially ignited parallel impacts in other areas of its business capacities among its subsidiaries numbering about 46 across the globe.

4.5.4 Data Loss

All exploits resulted in losses. Ransomware resulted in data loss where victims showed reluctance to pay ransom. Password abuse which led to user account compromise resulted in data theft and imposed huge costs in lost data. Malware action and cyber espionage resulted in data destruction and impacted logistics that led to loss of client patronage and exposure of confidential information.

4.5.5 Reputation Damage

The reputation of an organization is a cherished asset, and therefore, nothing could be as damaging as the scandal that follows a cybercrime, especially high-profile incidents involving multiple threats and exploits.

Firstly, it gives the initial impression of unpreparedness and poor Cybersecurity culture, which could affect trust levels from customers who have entrusted their data unto the organization in confidence. Secondly, it raises suspicions of insider collaboration which puts the brand, products, services, and reputation of the organization at great risk, and potentially affects its market competitiveness. Thirdly, the litigation and investigations that follow a cybercrime could be scandalous and could potentially reveal hidden secrets, which could further diminish the credibility of the organization.

For social networking organizations, e-commerce companies, and online retail stores, a hack could be as devastating as having to start afresh to rebuild customer database and attract fresh clientele by offering costly incentives [1] to the customers or business partners in an effort to maintain relationships and retain brand loyalty after the breach, a situation that could get worse if the incident becomes repeated in quick succession.

The Twitter incident of 15th July, 2020, where multiple high-profile user accounts belonging to Joe Biden Bill Gates, Barack Obama, Elon Musk, and 127 others were hacked, created suspicion in the minds of millions of its global customers, led to an almost instant dwindling of patronage of the microblogging and social networking giant, and caused a 4% drop in its shares within hours of the incident [190–192].

A breach in Twitter's security that allowed hackers to break into the accounts of influential leaders, technology moguls, and business executives shook trust in a platform which politicians and CEOs use to communicate with the public [193], and especially raised questions of insider collusion [194]. In what appeared like a demonstration of high-level distrust, the President Donald Trump avoided using Twitter to announce the demotion of his 2020 campaign manager, Brad Parscale [195, 196] just moments after the hack, and chose to use Facebook instead.

In the financial and healthcare industries, the loss of credit cards, banking credentials or medical records through Cybersecurity breaches could have an overbearing impact on the overall outlook of bank customers and patients, respectively, with a mindset of distrust over the online safety of their financial transactions and sensitive medical data. The alleged leak of about 230,000 COVID-19 test takers results [8] from Indonesian Government's database in May 2020 raised concerns over government's reputation in the management of citizen's data.

4.5.6 Revenue Loss

In addition to non-financial, logistic and operational hiccups, a cyberattack almost always comes with heavy financial losses. Such economic losses usually spread among cost of carrying out Cybersecurity incident response and recovery operations, loss due to dwindling income as a result of customers' withdrawal of patronage, cost incurred from the worth of stolen information or the value of damaged data.

For example, in the 15th July Twitter high-profile accounts hack, the actual and the perceived commercial losses that arose from the coordinated social engineering attack and phone scam [108] that targeted some of the Twitter employees with access to internal systems and tools could have included:

- Qualitative cost of dwindling customer loyalty.
- Cost of optimizing Cybersecurity awareness among employees.
- Cost of withdrawing patronage from business associates.
- Cost of consultancy on computer incident response (CIR).
- Cost of reconfiguring systems suspected to have been affected by the attack.
- Cost of installation of additional protective and anomaly detection security systems.
- Cost of compliance with laws and regulations regarding privacy and data protection [1], including any fines.
- Cost of procurement and deployment of more intelligent incident prediction systems.
- Cost of recruitment and/or training of specialist staff to oversee Cybersecurity compliance in the aftermath of the incident.
- Cost of litigation, investigations, and remediation.

In addition to these, costs associated with protections, including insurance coverage [1], could add up to significant proportions. Cybersecurity insurance covers expenses for notification, credit monitoring, investigation, crisis management, public relations, and legal advice. In general, revenue losses for victims are synonymous with Cybersecurity breaches and could impose a perpetual impact on the organization or threaten its corporate survivability in the long run.

4.5.7 Service Disruption for Organizations

Perhaps one of the immediate consequences of a cyberattack on an organization's operations is business disruption, which could be minor, major, short-term, or long-term depending on the scope of the attack, its severity, and especially the immediate recovery approach adopted to mitigate its impact. Threats have overall ripple effects on operational disruption and business sustenance.

- For example, following the insider attack on the computer systems of Stradis Healthcare, the delivery of PPE and other medical supplies was interrupted for several days [168, 169] to enable the company to contain the former employee's actions, limit further infiltration and recover what was left from the records modified or deleted by the attacker.

4.5.8 Service Disruption for Individuals

On an individual level, the impacts of a cyberattack could be even more devastating to the online safety of the victim, especially where private data has been exposed or confidential information compromised by a malicious hacker. The impacts can transcend from immediate interruption of online transactions to a more severe cyber espionage, cyber bullying, and online harassment on account of sensitive information that may have leaked into the wrong hands.

4.5.9 Crime Escalation

As it is hard to separate physical security from Cybersecurity, crime strives in an environment where security is either non-existent or inadequate. There were isolated COVID-19 induced environmental shortcomings that inadvertently promoted crime in the society resulting from poor security guarantees on physical data centres and other tangible assets. Cases of burglary attacks on computing installation were rife as criminals took advantages of the lockdown confusion to escalate crime incidents.

4.5.10 Fatality

Extreme cases of cyberattacks involving loss of, or delayed access to, critical life-saving information among healthcare facilities and medical institutions resulted in deaths. Such fatalities resulted due to the effects of cyber threats that caused damage or unauthorized alteration of medical data, including patients' PII and PHI and led to lack of, or inaccurate, information for prompt decision-making on emergency procedures, drug administration, hospitalization, and patient care.

4.6 CHAPTER SUMMARY

Elevated cyber risk levels characterized the COVID-19 pandemic, and accounted for the many sophisticated cybercrimes that took advantage of human, technical, and system vulnerabilities and resulted in far reaching impacts.

According to the FBI's 2019 Internet Crime Report [197], $3.5 billion was lost by individual and business victims to cybercrimes in 2019, a figure that rose by 29.6% over 2018's $2.7 billion [198, 199]. As these numbers continue to record yearly growth, the peculiarities of COVID-19 are expected to push the figures even higher in exponential proportions for 2020.

The components of these losses include ransoms paid to cyberattackers, fines paid to regulatory authorities, money paid for system updates and repairs, and the costs associated with lost clients and diminished business reputation [200]. The elevated cyber risk levels characterized the COVID-19 pandemic, accounted for the many sophisticated cybercrimes that took advantage of human, technical, and system vulnerabilities and compromised assets in the cyberspace, which eventually exerted various degrees of impacts on organizations and individuals. The impacts included identity theft, reputational damage, privacy infringements, and unauthorized modification of sensitive data.

Theft of sensitive and confidential data from organizations generally impacted customer patronage and market competitiveness, and particularly in the healthcare sector, where data loss undermined the efforts to contain the spread of the virus, and to provide adequate care to those directed affected.

The ability of the coronavirus disease to rapidly infect more people across many countries outside the epicentre of the outbreak made the nature and magnitude of the virus peculiar in comparison with the previous health emergencies of global dimension such as the 2014 Ebola virus outbreak. With such a peculiarity, it was very natural that humans would be desperately hungry for the information that could lead to the pandemic's control and eradication albeit out of despair, confusion, and desperation.

Such desperation resulted in the panic and anxiety that characterized the initial digital behaviour, which gave rise to increased online vulnerabilities that eventually ignited a wave of cyberattack exposures to social engineering. Cyber criminals capitalized on the uncertainty of the situation as well as human fear and apprehension to distribute destructive codes in the guise of authentic coronavirus information and stole confidential data in the process. The most proffered reasons for threat exploitations were identified to include the following:

- Employee ignorance.
- Social engineering campaign.
- Unpatched software.
- Insider collusion.
- System failure.
- Non-state actors [201].
- Technical errors.
- Disgruntled employees.
- Natural disaster.
- Issues with remote work from home.
- Hacking group, etc.

REFERENCES

1. C. Hoang, G. Tygesson and B. Cattanach, *"Cybersecurity risk factors: SEC guidance on cybersecurity disclosure and policies,"* Dorsey & Whitney LLP, Minneapolis, Minnesota, 2018.
2. Makin Paul, *"Digital identity: Issue analysis,"* Consult Hyperion, New York, 2016.
3. K. U. Okereafor and O. Adebola, "Tackling the cybersecurity impacts of the coronavirus outbreak as a challenge to internet safety," *International Journal in IT and Engineering (IJITE)*, vol. 8, no. 2, pp. 1–14, 2020.
4. K. Okereafor and O. Adelaiye, "Randomized cyber attack simulation model: A cybersecurity mitigation proposal for post COVID-19 digital era," *International Journal of Recent Engineering Research and Development (IJRERD)*, vol. 05, no. 07, pp. 61–72, 2020.

5. J. Menn, K. Paul and M. Hosenball, "U.S. Lawmakers Call for Explanation after Widespread Twitter Hack," Global News, 16 July 2020. [Online]. Available: https://globalnews.ca/news/7183428/twitter-stock-drops-hackers/ [Accessed 31 July 2020].

6. Akshay Bhargava, "In the New," Malwarebytes, 16 March 2020. [Online]. Available: https://press.malwarebytes.com/category/in-the-news/ [Accessed 30 July 2020].

7. Zak Doffman, "Hackers Attack Microsoft Windows Users: Dangerous Threat Group Exploits 'COVID-19 Fear'," Forbes, 16 March 2020. [Online]. Available: https://www.forbes.com/sites/zakdoffman/2020/03/16/this-dangerous-microsoft-windows-attack-exploits-covid-19-fear-governments-now-on-alert/#29e96b0742de [Accessed 30 July 2020].

8. News Desk, "Hacker Allegedly Breaches Govt Database on COVID-19 Test-takers," The Jakarta Post, 21 June 2020. [Online]. Available: https://www.thejakartapost.com/news/2020/06/20/hacker-allegedly-breaches-govt-data-base-on-covid-19-test-takers.html [Accessed 31 July 2020].

9. Lindal Yulisman, "Indonesia Probes Alleged Hacking of Covid-19 Test Data, SE Asia News," The Straits Times, 21 June 2020. [Online]. Available: https://www.straitstimes.com/asia/se-asia/indonesia-probes-alleged-hack-of-covid-19-test-data [Accessed 14 August 2020].

10. "San Francisco Airport Data Breach: Double Website Hack may have Lifted Users' Windows Login Credentials," The Daily Swig, 14 April 2020. [Online]. Available: https://portswigger.net/daily-swig/san-francisco-airport-data-breach-double-website-hack-may-have-lifted-users-windows-login-credentials [Accessed 1 August 2020].

11. T. Dargahi, A. Dehghantanha and P. Nikkhah, "A cyber-kill-chain based taxonomy of crypto-ransomware features," *Journal of Computer Virology and Hacking Techniques*, vol. 15, pp. 277–305 (https://doi.org/10.1007/s11416-019-00338-7), 2019.

12. Michael J. Assante and Robert M. Lee, *"The industrial control system cyber kill chain,"* SANS Institute, Maryland, US, 2015.

13. "Zoom Tackles Hackers with New Security Measures," BBC New, 6 June 2020. [Online]. Available: https://www.bbc.com/news/technology-52560602 [Accessed 16 August 2020].

14. Jane Wakefield, "Zoom Boss Apologises for Security Issues and Promises Fixes," BBC News, 2 April 2020. [Online]. Available: https://www.bbc.com/news/technology-52133349 [Accessed 16 August 2020].

15. "Coronavirus: Teachers in Singapore Stop Using Zoom after 'Lewd' Incidents," BBC News, 10 April 2020. [Online]. Available: https://www.bbc.com/news/world-asia-52240251 [Accessed 16 August 2020].

16. Christina Fan, "Concerns Growing Over Zoom Bombing As Hackers Interrupt Meetings," CBSN New York, 3 April 2020. [Online]. Available: https://newyork.cbslocal.com/2020/04/03/zoom-bombing-hackers-hijacking/ [Accessed 16 August 2020].

17. Steven Morris, "Zoom Hacker Streams Child Sex Abuse Footage to Plymouth Children," The Guardian, 7 May 2020. [Online]. Available: https://www.theguardian.com/society/2020/may/07/zoom-hacker-streams-child-sex-abuse-footage-to-plymouth-children [Accessed 16 August 2020].

18. Michael Kan, "Zoom Faces Lawsuit Over Bible Study Zoom-Bombing Incident," PC Mag, 14 May 2020. [Online]. Available: https://www.pcmag.com/news/zoom-faces-lawsuit-over-bible-study-zoom-bombing-incident [Accessed 16 August 2020].

19. Anthony Spadafora, "'Zoom-bombing' is Now a Federal Offense in the US," Tech Radar, 6 April 2020. [Online]. Available: https://www.techradar.com/news/zoom-bombing-is-now-a-federal-offense-in-the-us [Accessed 16 August 2020].

20. Alex Scroxton, "Zoom Making Progress on Cyber Security and Privacy, says CEO," Computer Weekly, 1 July 2020. [Online]. Available: https://www.computerweekly.com/news/252485510/Zoom-making-progress-on-cyber-security-and-privacy-says-CEO [Accessed 16 August 2020].

21. Alex Scroxton, "Zoom Buys Secure Messaging Service Keybase," Computer Weekly, 7 May 2020. [Online]. Available: https://www.computerweekly.com/news/252482833/Zoom-buys-secure-messaging-service-Keybase [Accessed 16 Auguat 2020].

22. Ari Levy, "Zoom buys Keybase — Its First Acquisition — as Part of 90-day Plan to Fix Security Flaws," CNBC, 7 May 2020. [Online]. Available: https://www.cnbc.com/2020/05/07/zoom-buys-keybase-in-first-deal-as-part-of-plan-to-fix-security.html [Accessed 16 August 2020].

23. Jacob Kastrenakes, "Zoom Buys the Identity Service Keybase as Part of 90-day Security Push," The Verge, 7 May 2020. [Online]. Available: https://www.theverge.com/2020/5/7/21250418/zoom-keybase-acquisition-encryption-security-messages-services [Accessed 16 August 2020].

24. Rob Sobers, "110 Must-Know Cybersecurity Statistics for 2020," Varonis, 21 July 2020. [Online]. Available: https://www.varonis.com/blog/cybersecurity-statistics/ [Accessed 31 July 2020].

25. Eric Cole, "The Top 5 Qualities of a Cybersecurity Expert Witness," Secure Anchor, 20 March 2020. [Online]. Available: https://www.secure-anchor.com/the-top-5-qualities-of-a-cybersecurity-expert-witness/ [Accessed 28 May 2020].

26. J. Hong, T. Kim, J. Liu, N. Park and S.-W. Kim, "Phishing URL detection with Lexical features and blacklisted domains," in Adaptive autonomous secure cyber systems, Springer, Cham, 2020, pp. 253–267.

27. United Nations Office on Drugs & Crime (UNODC), "COVID-19: Cyber Threat Analysis," Cybercrime Program, UNODC Middle East and North Africa (MENA) Assessment & Actions, Cairo, 2020.

28. K. Okereafor and A. Marcelo, "Addressing cybersecurity challenges of health data in the COVID-19 pandemic," International Journal in IT & Engineering, vol. 8, no. 6, pp. 1–12, 2020.

29. World Health Organizatio, "Report of the WHO-China Joint Mission on Coronavirus Disease 2019 (COVID-19)," World Health Organization, Geneva, 2020.

30. Lily Hay Newman, "The Covid-19 Pandemic Reveals Ransomware's Long Game," WIRED, 20 April 2020. [Online]. Available: https://www.wired.com/story/covid-19-pandemic-ransomware-long-game/ [Accessed 17 May 2020].

31. A. Kurniawan and I. Riadi, "Detection and analysis cerber ransomware based on network forensics behavior," International Journal of Network Security, vol. 20, no. 5, pp. 836–843, 2018.

32. K. Okereafor and R. Djehaiche, "A review of application challenges of digital forensics," *International Journal of Simulation Systems Science and Technology*, vol. 21, no. 2, pp. 35.1–35.7, 2020.

33. M. Akbanov, V. G. Vassilakis and M. D. Logothetis, "WannaCry ransomware: Analysis of infection, persistence, recovery prevention and propagation mechanisms," *Journal of Telecomminucations and Information Technology*, vol. 1, no. 2019, pp. 113–124, 2019.

34 E. Berrueta, D. Morato, E. Magaña and M. Izal, "A Survey on Detection Techniques for Cryptographic Ransomware," in IEEE Access, vol. 7, pp. 144925-144944, 2019, doi: 10.1109/ACCESS.2019.2945839.

35. David Ferbrache, "The Rise of Ransomware During COVID-19: How to Adapt to the New Threat Environment," KPMG, May 2020. [Online]. Available: https://home.kpmg/xx/en/home/insights/2020/05/rise-of-ransomware-during-covid-19.html [Accessed 17 May 2020].

36. A. K. Maurya, N. Kumar, A. Agrawal and R. Khan, "Ransomware: Evolution, target and safety measures," *International Journal of Computer Sciences and Engineering*, vol. 6, no. 1, pp. 80–85, 2018.

37. "BadRabbit Ransomware: Real-time report," Allot Communications, 2017.

38. "BadRabbit Ransomware," ThaiCERT, Bangkok, 2017.

39. S. K. Sahi, "A study of WannaCry ransomware attack," *International Journal of Engineering Research in Computer Science and Engineering (IJERCSE)*, vol. 4, no. 9, pp. 5–7, 2017.

40. Sharda Tickoo, "Demystifying Ransomware - the Cyber Pandemic," Economic Times, 29 June 2020. [Online]. Available: https://ciso.economictimes.india-times.com/news/demystifying-ransomware-the-cyber-pandemic/76684165 [Accessed 1 July 2020].

41. Sead Fadilpašić, "Data of over 500m Weibo Users for Sale on the Web," IT Pro Portal, 23 March 2020. [Online]. Available: https://www.itproportal.com/news/data-of-over-500m-weibo-users-for-sale-on-the-web/ [Accessed 17 August 2020].

42. Shuyano Kong, "How Weibo's Massive Privacy Breach affects China's Crypto Community," Decrypt, 22 March 2020. [Online]. Available: https://decrypt.co/23197/how-weibos-massive-privacy-breach-affects-chinas-crypto-community [Accessed 17 August 2020].

43. "500 Million Accounts of Weibo Leaked for Pennies in Darkweb – Data Posted for Sale," Cyble Inc., 1 June 2020. [Online]. Available: https://cybleinc.com/2020/06/01/500-million-accounts-of-weibo-leaked-for-pennies-in-dark-web-data-posted-for-sale/?__cf_chl_captcha_tk__=78bc10a076a8e2a4f72e6 c5def6be7f33a019620-1597700076-0-AR03-fL_mllpUOkjcVrRD9Js937md-4SJpho1zbqBCUHULY4JRcG4ajbvwzZfVlsQB [Accessed 17 August 2020].

44. Malcolm Moore, "China Moves to Control Sina Weibo Social Network with Real Names," The Telegraph, 16 March 2012. [Online]. Available: https://www.telegraph.co.uk/technology/news/9147767/China-moves-to-control-Sina-Weibo-social-network.html [Accessed 17 August 2020].

45. Zhang Yushuo, "China's IT Ministry Takes Sina Weibo to Task Over 538-Million User Data Leak," Yicai Global, 25 March 2020. [Online]. Available: https://www.yicaiglobal.com/news/china-it-ministry-takes-sina-weibo-to-task-over-538-million-user-data-leak [Accessed 17 August 2020].

46. Anandi Chandrashekhar, "Cognizant Hit by 'Maze' Ransomware Attack," *Economic Times*, 21 April 2020. [Online]. Available: https://economictimes. indiatimes.com/tech/internet/cognizant-hit-by-maze-ransomware-attack/ articleshow/75228505.cms?from=mdr [Accessed 22 June 2020].

47. The News Minute, "Cognizant Ransomware Attack: Credit Card Info, Personal Data of Some Employees Leaked," *The News Minute*, 22 June 2020. [Online]. Available: https://www.thenewsminute.com/article/cognizant-ransomware-attack-credit-card-info-personal-data-some-employees-leaked-127076 [Accessed 22 June 2020].

48. Lifars, "Cognizant Hacked by Maze Ransomware Attack," Lifars, 5 May 2020. [Online]. Available: https://lifars.com/2020/05/cognizant-hacked-by-maze-ransomware-attack/ [Accessed 22 June 2020].

49. Laura Dyrda, "Ransomware Attackers Hit 2 Providers, Post Patient Information and Photos Online: 5 details," *Becker's Hospital Review*, 7 May 2020. [Online]. Available: https://www.beckershospitalreview.com/cybersecurity/ransomware-attackers-hit-2-providers-post-patient-information-and-photos-online-5-details.html [Accessed 30 July 2020].

50. Bradley Barth, "No Reprieve for Health Care Orgs as Ransomware Hits Hospital Operator, Plastic Surgeons," *SC Media*, 6 May 2020. [Online]. Available: https://www.scmagazine.com/home/security-news/ransomware/no-reprieve-for-health-care-orgs-as-ransomware-hits-hospital-operator-plastic-surgeons/ [Accessed 30 July 2020].

51. Jessica Davis, "Maze Ransomware Hackers Post Patient Data Stolen from 2 Providers," *Health IT Security*, 6 May 2020. [Online]. Available: https:// healthitsecurity.com/news/maze-ransomware-hackers-post-patient-data-stolen-from-2-providers [Accessed 30 July 2020].

52. Dissent, "So Much for Their Moratorium on Attacking Healthcare Entities: Maze Team Attacks a Plastic Surgeon," *Data Breaches*, 5 May 2020. [Online]. Available: https://www.databreaches.net/so-much-for-their-moratorium-on-attacking-health-care-entities-maze-team-attacks-a-plastic-surgeon/ [Accessed 30 July 2020].

53. Eric Cole Dr., *"Phishing: You Are A Target,"* Secure Anchor Consulting, Ashburn, VA, 2020.

54. Paolo Passeri, "1-15 May 2020 Cyber Attacks Timeline," HACKMAGEDDON: Information Security Timelines and Statistics, 19 June 2020. [Online]. Available: https://www.hackmageddon.com/2020/06/19/1-15-may-2020-cyber-attacks-timeline/ [Accessed 30 July 2020].

55. Brian Krebs, "Europe's Largest Private Hospital Operator Fresenius Hit by Ransomware," Krebs on Security, 6 May 2020. [Online]. Available: https:// krebsonsecurity.com/2020/05/europes-largest-private-hospital-operator-fresenius-hit-by-ransomware/ [Accessed 30 July 2020].

56. Huang Yan Fen, "[Exclusive] Garmin is Suspected of being Attacked by Ransomware, the Production Line is Expected to be Shut Down for Two Days, and Mobile App Updates cannot be Synchronized," iThome, 23 July 2020. [Online]. Available: https://archive.fo/VZhk9#selection-1471.178-1471.198 [Accessed 23 August 2020].

57. Iain Treloar, "Garmin Suffers Global Outage after Suspected Ransomware Attack," CyclingTips, 24 July 2020. [Online]. Available: https://cyclingtips.com/2020/07/ garmin-global-outage-ransomware-attack/ [Accessed 3 August 2020].

58. Matt de Neef, "How did the Garmin Cyber Attack Happen, and What does It mean for Users?," CyclingTips, 30 July 2020. [Online]. Available: https://cyclingtips.com/2020/07/how-did-the-garmin-cyber-attack-happen-and-what-does-it-mean-for-users/ [Accessed 3 August 2020].

59. Robert W. Wood, "Garmin hack's $10M Ransom Payment, $10M Tax Deduction," Forbes, 27 July 2020. [Online]. Available: https://www.forbes.com/sites/robertwood/2020/07/27/garmin-hacks-10m-ransom-payment-10m-tax-deduction/#2647948412c5 [Accessed 3 August 2020].

60. "Garmin Home Page," Garmin, 3 August 2020. [Online]. Available: https://www.garmin.com/en-US/ [Accessed 3 August 2020].

61. Lawrence Abrams, "Confirmed: Garmin received Decryptor for WastedLocker Ransomware," BleepingComputer, 1 August 2020. [Online]. Available: https://www.bleepingcomputer.com/news/security/confirmed-garmin-received-decryptor-for-wastedlocker-ransomware/ [Accessed 3 August 2020].

62. Alicia Hope, "Ransomware Attack on Garmin services Leaves Pilots and Users Unable to Operate," CPO Magazine, 30 July 2020. [Online]. Available: https://www.cpomagazine.com/cyber-security/ransomware-attack-on-garmin-services-leaves-pilots-and-users-unable-to-operate/ [Accessed 3 August 2020].

63. Philip Muncaster, "Garmin Outage could Ground Aircraft," Info Security, 24 July 2020. [Online]. Available: https://www.infosecurity-magazine.com/news/garmin-outage-could-ground [Accessed 3 August 2020].

64. Dan Raywood, "Garmin Confirms Cyber-attack as Ransomware Recovery Rumored," Info Security Magazine, 28 July 2020. [Online]. Available: https://www.infosecurity-magazine.com/news/garmin-attack-ransomware/ [Accessed 3 August 2020].

65. Jeff Stone, "Garmin Confirms Ransomware Attack, Keeps Quiet on Possible Evil Corp. Involvement," CyberScoop, 27 July 2020. [Online]. Available: https://www.cyberscoop.com/garmin-ransomware-attack-evil-corp-wasted-locker/ [Accessed 3 August 2020].

66. Tomas Meskauskas, "Evil Corp's WastedLocker Demanding Millions of Dollars for Decryption," Security Boulevard, 17 July 2020. [Online]. Available: https://securityboulevard.com/2020/07/evil-corps-wastedlocker-demanding-millions-of-dollars-for-decryption/ [Accessed 3 August 2020].

67. Brian Barrett, "Alleged Russian Hacker behind $100 Million Evil Corp Indicted," Wired, 2019. [Online]. Available: https://www.wired.com/story/alleged-russian-hacker-evil-corp-indicted/ [Accessed 3 August 2020].

68. "Russian Hacker Group Evil Corp Targets US Workers at Home," BBC News, 26 June 2020. [Online]. Available: https://www.bbc.com/news/world-us-canada-53195749 [Accessed 3 August 2020].

69. Andrew Martonik, "Garmin Services Restored after Multi-day Cyber Attack: Details and Next Steps," Android Central, 27 July 2020. [Online]. Available: https://www.androidcentral.com/garmin-connect-suffers-multi-hour-outage [Accessed 3 August 2020].

70. Joe Tidy, "Garmin Begins Recovery from Ransomware Attack," BBC News, 27 July 2020. [Online]. Available: https://www.bbc.com/news/technology-53553576 [Accessed 3 August 2020].

71. Adam Ruggiero, "Garmin Hacked in Massive Ransomware Attack: Service Returns to Normal," Gear Junkie, 28 July 2020. [Online]. Available: https://gearjunkie.com/garmin-hacked-evil-corp-ransomware [Accessed 3 August 2020].

72. Caleb Chen, "The Garmin Hack could have been a Disastrous, Large Scale Privacy Breach," Privacy News Online, 29 July 2020. [Online]. Available: https://www.privateinternetaccess.com/blog/the-garmin-hack-could-have-been-a-disastrous-large-scale-privacy-breach/ [Accessed 3 August 2020].

73. Brian Barrett, "The Garmin Hack was a Warning," Wired, July 2020. [Online]. Available: https://www.wired.com/story/garmin-ransomware-hack-warning/ [Accessed 3 August 2020].

74. Security Lab, "Clop, Clop! It's a TA505 HTML Malspam Analysis," Hornet Security, 7 July 2020. [Online]. Available: https://www.hornetsecurity.com/en/security-information/clop-clop-ta505-html-malspam-analysis/#:~:text=the%20Clop%20ransomware.-,Clop%20ransomware,stage%20of%20an%20TA505%20attack [Accessed 28 July 2020].

75. Ross Brewer, "Ransomware attacks: Detection, prevention and cure," *Network Security*, vol. 2016, no. 9, pp. 5–9, 2016.

76. Sean O'Kane, "Honda Pauses Production and Closes Offices Following Ransomware Attack," The Verge, 9 June 2020. [Online]. Available: https://www.theverge.com/2020/6/9/21285758/honda-ransomware-virus-attack-production-halt-offices-workers [Accessed 19 August 2020].

77. Adam Smith, "Honda Cyber Attack: Factories across World Brought to Standstill by Ransomware Hack," Independent, 9 June 2020. [Online]. Available: https://www.independent.co.uk/life-style/gadgets-and-tech/news/honda-cyber-attack-ransomware-computer-email-server-uk-india-brazil-a9557071.html [Accessed 19 August 2020].

78. Tovey Alan and Cook James, "Honda could be Victim of Ransomware Cyber Attack," The Telegraph, 8 June 2020. [Online]. Available: https://www.telegraph.co.uk/business/2020/06/08/honda-could-victim-ransomware-cyber-attack/ [Accessed 19 August 2020].

79. Zack Whittaker, "Honda Global Operations Halted by Ransomware Attack," TechCrunch, 9 June 2020. [Online]. Available: https://techcrunch.com/2020/06/09/honda-ransomware-snake/ [Accessed 19 August 2020].

80. Davey Winder, "Honda Hacked: Japanese Car Giant Confirms Cyber Attack on Global Operations," Forbes, 10 June 2020. [Online]. Available: https://www.forbes.com/sites/daveywinder/2020/06/10/honda-hacked-japanese-car-giant-confirms-cyber-attack-on-global-operations-snake-ransomware/#436fb56653ad [Accessed 19 August 2020].

81. Joe Tidy, "Honda's Global Operations Hit by Cyber-attack," BBC News, 9 June 2020. [Online]. Available: https://www.bbc.com/news/technology-52982427 [Accessed 19 August 2020].

82. Jai Vijayan, "WannaCry Forces Honda to Take Production Plant Offline," Dark Reading, 21 June 2017. [Online]. Available: https://www.darkreading.com/attacks-breaches/wannacry-forces-honda-to-take-production-plant-offline-/d/d-id/1329192 [Accessed 19 August 2020].

83. "Honda Halts Japan Car Plant after WannaCry Virus Hits Computer Network," Reuters, 21 June 2017. [Online]. Available: https://www.reuters.com/article/us-honda-cyberattack/honda-halts-japan-car-plant-after-wannacry-virus-hits-computer-network-idUSKBN19C0EI [Accessed 19 August 2020].

84. Peter Lyon, "Cyber Attack at Honda Stops Production after WannaCry Worm Strikes," Forbes, 22 June 2017. [Online]. Available: https://www.forbes.com/sites/peterlyon/2017/06/22/cyber-attack-at-honda-stops-production-after-wannacry-worm-strikes/#66e049395e2b [Accessed 19 August 2020].

85. Ben Dooley and Hisako Ueno, "Honda Hackers May Have Used Tools Favored by Countries," The New York Times, 12 June 2020. [Online]. Available: https://www.nytimes.com/2020/06/12/business/ransomware-honda-hacking-factories.html#:~:text=A%20computer%20virus%20hit%20the,from%20email%20or%20internal%20servers [Accessed 19 August 2020].

86. Maki Shiraki and Naomi Tajitsu, "Honda Resumes Production at Plants Hit by Cyberattack," Automative News, 12 June 2020. [Online]. Available: https://www.autonews.com/manufacturing/honda-resumes-production-plants-hit-cyberattack [Accessed 19 August 2020].

87. "Honda Resumes Production at Plants Hit by Suspected Cyber Attack," Reuters, 12 June 2020. [Online]. Available: https://www.reuters.com/article/us-honda-cyber/honda-resumes-production-at-plants-hit-by-suspected-cyber-attack-idUSKBN23J0ND [Accessed 19 August 2020].

88. Sonali Jadha, "Spyware and trojan horses," *International Journal for Scientific Research & Development (IJSRD)*, vol. 5, no. 8, pp. 94–99, 2017.

89. Zhu Zhenfang, "Study on computer Trojan horse virus and its prevention," *International Journal of Engineering and Applied Sciences (IJEAS)*, vol. 2, no. 8, pp. 95–96, 2015.

90. J. Machteld, *Mellink, Troy and the Trojan War: A symposium held at Bryn Mawr College, October 1984*, Bryn Mawr College Publications, Bryn Mawr, Pennsylvania, 1986.

91. Michael Trapp, *Troy and the True Story of the Trojan War*, Kings College London, London, 1997.

92. M. I. Finley, J. L. Caskey, G. S. Kirk and D. L. Page, "The Trojan war," *The Journal of Hellenic Studies*, vol. 84, no. https://doi.org/10.2307/627688, pp. 1–20, 1964.

93. Akshaya Asokan, "Enhanced Zeus Sphinx Trojan Used in COVID-19 Schemes," Bank Info Security, 12 May 2020. [Online]. Available: https://www.bankinfosecurity.com/enhanced-zeus-sphinx-trojan-used-in-covid-19-schemes-a-14267 [Accessed 2 August 2020].

94. Tara Seals, "Brazil's Banking Trojans Go Global," Threat Post, 15 July 2020. [Online]. Available: https://threatpost.com/brazils-banking-trojans-global/157452/ [Accessed 2 August 2020].

95. Seans Lyngaas, "Attackers are Using a Brazilian Hacking Tool against Spanish Banks," CYBERSCOOP, 14 April 2020. [Online]. Available: https://www.cyberscoop.com/attackers-using-brazilian-hacking-tool-spanish-banks/ [Accessed 2 August 2020].

96. "The Trojan Grandoreiro uses COVID-19 to Make a Comeback and Start Attacking Banks," Cytomic, 20 May 2020. [Online]. Available: https://www.cytomic.ai/alerts/trojan-grandoreiro-attack-banks/ [Accessed 2 August 2020].

97. James Coker, "Researchers Spot Banking Trojan Using #COVID19 Crisis to Attack Users," Information Security, 28 April 2020. [Online]. Available: https://www.infosecurity-magazine.com/news/banking-trojan-covid-attack/ [Accessed 2 August 2020].

98. D. Frank, L. Rochberger, Y. Rimmer and A. Dahan, "EventBot: A New Mobile Banking Trojan is Born," Cybereason Nocturnus, 30 April 2020. [Online]. Available: https://www.cybereason.com/blog/eventbot-a-new-mobile-banking-trojan-is-born [Accessed 19 August 2020].

99. IANS, "Beware of Mobile Banking Malware EventBot, Warns CERT-In," Express Computer, 18 May 2020. [Online]. Available: https://www.express-computer.in/egov-watch/beware-of-mobile-banking-malware-eventbot-warns-cert-in/55942/ [Accessed 2 September 2020].

100. David García, "EventBot, A New Family of Banking Malware for Android," Buguroo, March 2020. [Online]. Available: https://www.buguroo.com/en/labs/eventbot-a-new-family-of-banking-malware-for-android [Accessed 2 September 2020].

101. Zack Whittaker, "Meet EventBot, a New Android Malware that Steals Banking Passwords and Two-factor Codes," Tech Crunch, 30 April 2020. [Online]. Available: https://techcrunch.com/2020/04/29/eventbot-android-malware-banking/ [Accessed 19 August 2020].

102. Cybereason, "Threat Alert: EventBot Mobile Trojan," Cybereason, Boston, Massachusetts, 2020.

103. David Bisson, "Cerberus Android Malware Gains Ability to Steal 2FA Tokens, Screen Lock Credentials," Security Intelligence, 2 March 2020. [Online]. Available: https://securityintelligence.com/news/cerberus-android-malware-gains-ability-to-steal-2fa-tokens-screen-lock-credentials/ [Accessed 19 August 2020].

104. Financial Express Online, "Beware of Potentially Dangerous Banking Trojan 'Cerberus' exploiting COVID-19 Crisis: CBI," Financial Express, 19 May 2020. [Online]. Available: https://www.financialexpress.com/industry/technology/beware-of-potentially-dangerous-banking-trojan-cerberus-exploiting-covid-19-crisis-cbi/1964269/ [Accessed 2 August 2020].

105. Arvind Gunasekar, "Cyber Virus Stealing Credit Card Details Using COVID-19 Information: CBI," NDTV, 19 May 2020. [Online]. Available: https://www.ndtv.com/india-news/cerberus-coronavirus-malicious-software-stealing-financial-data-using-covid-information-cbi-2231652 [Accessed 19 August 2020].

106. Patrick Nohe, "5 Ways to Determine if a Website is Fake, Fraudulent, or a Scam – 2018," The SSL Store, 2 November 2018. [Online]. Available: https://www.thesslstore.com/blog/5-ways-to-determine-if-a-website-is-fake-fraudulent-or-a-scam/ [Accessed 12 June 2020].

107. "Top 6 Common Types of Cyberattacks in 2020," DNS Stuff, 12 May 2020. [Online]. Available: https://www.dnsstuff.com/common-types-of-cyber-attacks [Accessed 1 August 2020].

108. Press Trust of India (PTI) Agency, "Twitter says hackers used phone to fool staff, gain access," CISO Economic Times, 31 July 2020. [Online]. Available: https://ciso.economictimes.indiatimes.com/news/twitter-says-hackers-used-phone-to-fool-staff-gain-access/77283939 [Accessed 1 August 2020].

109. Jessica Davis, "Hackers Using COVID-19 Phishing, Website Spoofing for Credential Theft," Health IT Security, 20 May 2020. [Online]. Available: https://healthitsecurity.com/news/hackers-using-covid-19-phishing-website-spoofing-for-credential-theft [Accessed 14 August 2020].

110. H. S. Lallie, L. A. Shepherd, J. R. C. Nurse, A. Erola, G. Epiphaniou, C. Maple and X. Bellekens, "Cyber security in the age of COVID-19: A timeline and analysis of cyber-crime and cyber-attacks during the pandemic," arXiv, vol. arXiv:2006.11929v1 [cs.CR], pp. 1–19, 2020.

111. Laura Dyrda, "BJC HealthCare Reports Employee Email Breach Exposes PHI for 19 Facilities: 5 Details," Becker's Health IT, 6 May 2020. [Online]. Available: https://www.beckershospitalreview.com/cybersecurity/bjc-healthcare-reports-employee-email-breach-exposes-phi-for-19-facilities-5-details.html [Accessed 2 September 2020].

112. BJC HealthCare, "Notice to Patients," BJC, 5 May 2020. [Online]. Available: https://www.bjc.org/Newsroom/Article/ArtMID/5522/ArticleID/4438/Notice-to-Patients [Accessed 30 July 2020].

113. Tim Sandle, "Australia: NSW Hit by Data Breach via Phishing Attack," Digital Journal, 16 May 2020. [Online]. Available: http://www.digitaljournal.com/tech-and-science/technology/australia-nsw-hit-by-data-breach-via-phishing-attack/article/571714 [Accessed 14 August 2020].

114. Asha Barbaschow, "Citizen Data Compromised as Service NSW Falls Victim to Phishing Attack," ZDNet, 14 May 2020. [Online]. Available: https://www.zdnet.com/article/citizen-data-compromised-as-service-nsw-falls-victim-to-phishing-attack/ [Accessed 14 August 2020].

115. Julia Talevski, "Service NSW Falls Victim to Phishing Attack," ARN, 14 May 2020. [Online]. Available: https://www.arnnet.com.au/article/679705/service-nsw-falls-victim-phishing-attack/ [Accessed 14 August 2020].

116. "Service NSW Cyber Incident," Service NSW, 2020. [Online]. Available: https://www.service.nsw.gov.au/cyber-incident [Accessed 14 August 2020].

117. Eoin Carroll, "Transitioning to a Mass Remote Workforce – We Must Verify Before Trusting," McAfee, 7 April 2020. [Online]. Available: https://www.mcafee.com/blogs/other-blogs/mcafee-labs/transitioning-to-a-mass-remote-workforce-we-must-verify-before-trusting/ [Accessed 17 May 2020].

118. Digital Watch, "Coronavirus Crisis: A Digital Policy Overview," Geneva Internet Platform Digital Watch, 2020. [Online]. Available: https://dig.watch/trends/coronavirus-crisis-digital-policy-overview#view-15663-5 [Accessed 18 May 2020].

119. Deloitte Cyber Threat Intelligence (CTI), "The Rise of Insider Threats Amid COVID-19," Deloitte, London, 2020.

120. Crist Ry and Wong Queenie, "Twitter Hack Hits Elon Musk, Obama, Kanye West, Bill Gates and More in Bitcoin Scam," CNET, 16 July 2020. [Online]. Available: https://www.cnet.com/news/coordinated-twitter-hack-hits-elon-musk-obama-kanye-west-bill-gates-and-more-in-bitcoin-scam/ [Accessed 20 July 2020].

121. S. Lewandowsky and J. Cook, *The Conspiracy Theory Handbook,* George Mason University, Virginia, Fairfax, 2020.

122. H. Allcott and M. Gentzkow, "Social media and fake News in the 2016 elections," *Journal of Economic Perspectives,* vol. 31, no. 2, pp. 211–236, 2017.

123. A. Joseph and H. Branswell, "Trump: U.S. will Terminate Relationship with the World Health Organization in Wake of Covid-19 Pandemic," STAT News, 29 May 2020. [Online]. Available: https://www.statnews.com/2020/05/29/trump-us-terminate-who-relationship/ [Accessed 30 July 2020].

124. Berkeley Lovelace Jr., "Trump Says the U.S. will Cut Ties with World Health Organization," CNBC HEALTH AND SCIENCE, 29 May 2020. [Online]. Available: https://www.cnbc.com/2020/05/29/trump-says-the-us-will-cut-ties-with-world-health-organization.html [Accessed 30 July 2020].

125. Kaiser Health News, "Trump Makes Official the U.S. Exit from World Health Organization," Kaiser Health News (KHN), 8 July 2020. [Online]. Available: https://khn.org/morning-breakout/trump-makes-official-the-u-s-exit-from-world-health-organization/ [Accessed 30 July 2020].

126. Z. Cohen, J. Hansler and K. Atwood, "Trump Administration Begins Formal Withdrawal from World Health Organization," CNN Politics, 8 July 2020. [Online]. Available: https://edition.cnn.com/2020/07/07/politics/us-withdrawing-world-health-organization/index.html [Accessed 30 July 2020].

127. Charles Creitz, "Rep. McCaul Praises Trump's WHO Withdrawal, Says 'They Have One Year to Get Their Act Together' withdrawal-China," Fox News, 7 July 2020. [Online]. Available: https://www.foxnews.com/media/mccaul-trump-world-health-organization-withdrawal-china [Accessed 30 July 2020].

128. Charlie Campbell, "'A Crime against Humanity.' Why Trump's WHO Funding Freeze Benefits Nobody," Time, 15 April 2020. [Online]. Available: https://time.com/5821122/who-funding-trump-covid19-coronavirus-china/ [Accessed 30 July 2020].

129. Gary Edson, "Abandoning the World Health Organization Will Benefit China," The National Interest, 8 June 2020. [Online]. Available: https://news.yahoo.com/abandoning-world-health-organization-benefit-233300615.html [Accessed 30 July 2020].

130. Will Hurd, "Leaving the W.H.O. Shows Poor Leadership," The New York Times, 29 May 2020. [Online]. Available: https://www.nytimes.com/2020/05/29/opinion/trump-who-world-health-organization.html [Accessed 30 July 2020].

131. Editorial, "Withholding Funding from the World Health Organization is Wrong and Dangerous, and Must Be Reversed," Nature, 17 April 2020. [Online]. Available: https://www.nature.com/articles/d41586-020-01121-1 [Accessed 30 July 2020].

132. Editorial, "Getting Out of the World Health Organization Might Not Be as Easy as Trump Thinks," Nature, 23 June 2020. [Online]. Available: https://www.nature.com/articles/d41586-020-01847-y [Accessed 30 July 2020].

133. A. Timsit and A. Shendruk, "Trump's Suspension of WHO Funding is a Disaster for the World's Health," Quartz, 15 April 2020. [Online]. Available: https://qz.com/1838378/what-you-need-to-know-about-trumps-suspension-of-who-funding/ [Accessed 30 July 2020].

134. Jessica Colarossi, "Why Withdrawing the United States from the WHO "Is a Terrible Decision"," The Brink: Boston University, 17 July 2020. [Online]. Available: http://www.bu.edu/articles/2020/why-withdrawing-the-united-states-from-the-who-is-a-terrible-decision/ [Accessed 30 July 2020].

135. B. Atkins and W. Huang, "A study of social engineering in online frauds," *Open Journal of Social Sciences*, vol. 1, no. 3, p. 23–2013.

136. E. Cole and S. Ring, "Insider Threat: Protecting the Enterprise from Sabotage," *Spying, and Theft*, Syngress Publishing Inc., Ashburn Virginia, 2006.

137. Nakamoto Satoshi, "Bitcoin: A Peer-to-Peer Electronic Cash System," 2008.

138. Barbara Ortutay, "Twitter: Hack Hit 130 Accounts, Company Embarrassed," AP News, 19 July 2020. [Online]. Available: https://apnews.com/860daee9d5 1ceb588c9bd0feebddc323#:~:text=OAKLAND%2C%20Calif.,of%2045%20 of%20those%20accounts [Accessed 21 July 2020].

139. Nick Statt, "Twitter Reveals That Its Own Employee Tools Contributed to Unprecedented Hack," The Verge, 15 July 2020. [Online]. Available: https://www.theverge.com/2020/7/15/21326656/twitter-hack-explanation-bitcoin-accounts-employee-tools [Accessed 21 July 2020].

140. Joseph Carson, "The Twitter Hack and the Failure to Protect Privileged Access," Thycotic, 17 July 2020. [Online]. Available: https://thycotic.com/company/blog/2020/07/17/twitter-hack-and-failure-to-protect-privileged-access/ [Accessed 21 July 2020].

141. "Florida Teenager Arrested over Twitter Account Cyber Attack," RTE, 31 July 2020. [Online]. Available: https://www.rte.ie/news/2020/0731/1156731-twitter-hack/ [Accessed 2 September 2020].

142. "Sophos 2020 Threat Report," Sophos, Abingdon, UK, 2020.

143. P. A. Grassi, J. L. Fenton, E. M. Newton, N. B. Lefkovitz and Y.-Y. Choong, *"Digital Identity Guidelines: Authentication and Lifecycle Management,"* National Institute of Standards and Technology (NIST) Special Publication 800-63B, Maryland, USA, 2017.

144. SANS Institute, *"Password Protection Policy,"* SANS Institute, Maryland, USA, 2017.

145. SANS Institute, *"Password Construction Guidelines,"* SANS Institute, Maryland, USA, 2017.

146. Ugo Onwuaso, "NITDA Cautions Nigerians on Fake Websites Pledging Federal Government Lockdown Funds," Nigeria Communications Week, 16 June 2020. [Online]. Available: https://www.nigeriacommunicationsweek.com.ng/nitda-cautions-nigerians-on-fake-websites-pledging-federal-government-lockdown-funds/ [Accessed 16 June 2020].

147. "Covid-19: No Federal Government Lockdown Funds, NITDA Alerts Nigerians on Fake Website," IT Pulse, 16 June 2020. [Online]. Available: https://itpulse.com.ng/2020/06/16/covid-19-no-federal-government-lockdown-funds-nitda-alerts-nigerians-on-fake-website/ [Accessed 14 August 2020].

148. Ruth Okwumbu, "NITDA Unmasks Fake Websites Disbursing 'Lockdown Funds'," Nairametrics, 16 June 2020. [Online]. Available: https://nairametrics.com/2020/06/16/nitda-unmasks-fake-websites-disbursing-lockdown-funds/ [Accessed 14 August 2020].

149. NCC Media Team, "DISCLAIMER - Press Statement: NCC Alerts Nigerians about Fake Website Spreading False Free Internet Claim," Nigerian Communications Commission (NCC), 2 April 2020. [Online]. Available: https://www.ncc.gov.ng/media-centre/news-headlines/809-disclaimer-press-statement-ncc-alerts-nigerians-about-fake-website-spreading-false-free-internet-claim [Accessed 14 August 2020].

150. "NCC Raises Alarm over 'Fake' Website Spreading False Free Internet Claim," TechEconomy, 2 April 2020. [Online]. Available: https://techeconomy.ng/2020/04/ncc-raises-alarm-over-fake-website-spreading-false-free-internet-claim/ [Accessed 14 August 2020].

151. Wale Odunsi, "COVID-19: NCC Warns Nigerians about Fake Website Offering Free Internet," Daily Post, 2 April 2020. [Online]. Available: https://dailypost.ng/2020/04/02/covid-19-ncc-warns-nigerians-about-fake-website-offering-free-internet/ [Accessed 14 August 2020].

152. Samson Echenim, "EFCC Alerts Nigerians on Fake Lockdown Funds," Business A. M., 28 April 2020. [Online]. Available: https://www.businessamlive.com/efcc-alerts-nigerians-on-fake-lockdown-funds/ [Accessed 14 August 2020].

153. Kris Ketz, "Some Fake COVID-19 Websites Could Hijack Your Computer with Just a Click," KMBC, 1 July 2020. [Online]. Available: https://www.kmbc.com/article/some-fake-covid-19-websites-could-hijack-your-computer-with-just-a-click/33041833 [Accessed 22 August 2020].

154. Duncan Riley, "Login Credentials Stolen in Hack of San Francisco International Airport Websites," Silicon Angle, 12 April 2020. [Online]. Available: https://siliconangle.com/2020/04/12/login-credentials-stolen-hack-san-francisco-international-airport-websites/ [Accessed 1 August 2020].

155. Davey Winder, "San Francisco Airport Cyber Attack Confirmed: Windows Passwords Stolen," Forbes, 11 April 2020. [Online]. Available: https://www.forbes.com/sites/daveywinder/2020/04/11/san-francisco-airport-cyber-attack-confirmed-windows-passwords-stolen/#608b75125b9c. [Accessed 31 July 2020].

156. Catalin Cimpanu, "Russian State Hackers Behind San Francisco Airport Hack," Zero Day, 14 April 2020. [Online]. Available: https://www.zdnet.com/article/russian-state-hackers-behind-san-francisco-airport-hack/ [Accessed 1 August 2020].

157. Abhilash, "Breaking down the San Francisco Airport Hack," Manage Engine IT Security, 22 April 2020. [Online]. Available: https://blogs.manageengine.com/it-security/2020/04/22/breaking-down-the-san-francisco-airport-hack.html [Accessed 31 July 2020].

158. San Fransisco International Airport, "Notice of Data Breach," 7 April 2020. [Online]. Available: http://media.flysfo.com.s3.amazonaws.com/pdf/Memo - Notice of Data Breach_il-4-3-2020_ntn.pdf [Accessed 3 August 2020].

159. Luke Irwin, "Avon's UK Website Offline a Week after Suffering Cyber Attack," IT Governance, 17 June 2020. [Online]. Available: https://www.itgovernance.co.uk/blog/avons-uk-website-offline-a-week-after-suffering-cyber-attack [Accessed 3 August 2020].

160. Alex Scroxton, "Cosmetics Company Avon Offline after Cyber Attack," Computer Weekly, 17 June 2020. [Online]. Available: https://www.computerweekly.com/news/252484804/Cosmetics-company-Avon-offline-after-cyberattack [Accessed 3 August 2020].

161. Phil Muncaster, "Cosmetics Giant Avon Leaks 19 Million Records," Info Security, 28 July 2020. [Online]. Available: https://www.infosecurity-magazine.com/news/cosmetics-giant-avon-leaks-19/ [Accessed 22 August 2020].

162. Alex Scroxton, "Cosmetics Firm Avon Faces New Cyber Security Incident," Computer Weekly, 29 July 2020. [Online]. Available: https://www.computerweekly.com/news/252486832/Cosmetics-firm-Avon-faces-new-cyber-security-incident [Accessed 22 August 2020].

163. Jim Wilson, "Cybersecurity Vulnerability at Major Cosmetics Brand Leads to 7 Gigabytes+ Data Leak," 28 July 2020. [Online]. Available: https://www.safetydetectives.com/blog/avon-leak-report/ [Accessed 22 August 2020].

164. Agnes Talalaev, "Website Hacking Statistics in 2020," WebARK, 23 July 2020. [Online]. Available: https://www.webarxsecurity.com/website-hacking-statistics-2018-february/ [Accessed 3 August 2020].

165. Marco Romagna, "Hacktivism: Conceptualization, techniques, and historical view," in *The Palgrave handbook of international cybercrime and cyberdeviance*, Palgrave Macmillan, Cham, 2020, pp. 743–769.

166. Dorothy E. Denning, "Activism, hacktivism, and cyberterrorism: The Internet as a tool for influencing foreign policy,"," in *Networks and netwars: The future of terror, crime, and militancy*, RAND, Santa Monica CA, 2001, pp. 239–288.

167. "FBI: Former Stradis VP Christopher Dobbins Charged With Sabotaging Shipments of PPE To Hospitals," CBS Atlanta, 17 April 2020. [Online]. Available: https://atlanta.cbslocal.com/2020/04/17/fbi-former-stradis-vp-christopher-dobbins-charged-with-sabotaging-shipments-of-ppe-to-hospitals/ [Accessed 23 August 2020].

168. Kate Brumback, "Man Accused of Causing Delay in Delivery of Health Equipment," ABC News, 16 April 2020. [Online]. Available: https://abcnews.go.com/Health/wireStory/man-accused-causing-delay-delivery-health-equipment-70193693 [Accessed 23 August 2020].

169. Zachary Hansen, "FBI: Scorned Ex-VP at Gwinnett Healthcare Company Sabotaged Shipments of Masks, Gloves," The Atlanta Journal-Constitution (AJC), 17 April 2020. [Online]. Available: https://www.ajc.com/news/crime–law/fbi-scorned-gwinnett-healthcare-company-sabotaged-shipments-masks-gloves/pXIKyuomUtRC9TeOodgOYI/ [Accessed 23 August 2020].

170. The Associated Press, "Man Admits Damaging Computer, Causing PPE Delivery Delay," ABC News, 10 July 2020. [Online]. Available: https://abcnews.go.com/Health/wireStory/man-admits-damaging-computer-causing-ppe-delivery-delay-71720106 [Accessed 23 August 2020].

171. "All On Georgia, Ga Man Pleads Guilty to Disrupting PPE Shipments by Damaging a computer," 13 July 2020. [Online]. Available: https://allongeorgia.com/georgia-public-safety/ga-man-pleads-guilty-to-disrupting-ppe-shipments-by-damaging-a-computer/ [Accessed 23 August 2020].

172. "Former Stradis VP Christopher Dobbins Pleads Guilty In Sabotaging Hospital PPE Shipments Case," News Break, 12 July 2020. [Online]. Available: https://www.newsbreak.com/news/1599220608338/former-stradis-vp-christopher-dobbins-pleads-guilty-in-sabotaging-hospital-ppe-shipments-case [Accessed 23 August 2020].

173. Ewdison Then, "Roblox Accounts Got Hacked by Allegedly Bribing an Insider [Updated]," Slash Gear, 4 May 2020. [Online]. Available: https://www.slashgear.com/roblox-accounts-got-hacked-by-allegedly-bribing-an-insider-04619242/ [Accessed 23 August 2020].

174. Joseph Cox, "Hacker Bribed 'Roblox' Insider to Access User Data," Motherboard, 4 May 2020. [Online]. Available: https://www.vice.com/en_us/article/qj4ddw/hacker-bribed-roblox-insider-accessed-user-data-reset-passwords [Accessed 23 August 2020].

175. Xeni Jardin, "Hacker Bribed and Phished to Access Some Roblox Accounts," BoingBoing, 4 May 2020. [Online]. Available: https://boingboing.net/2020/05/04/roblox-hacker-got-100-mill.html [Accessed 23 August 2020].

176. Aptoide App Store, "Aptiode Andriod Applications," Aptoide, 2020. [Online]. Available: https://en.aptoide.com/group/applications [Accessed 30 July 2020].

177. Paolo Passeri, "16-30 April 2020 Cyber Attacks Timeline," HACKMAGEDDON: Information Security Timelines and Statistics, 26 May 2020. [Online]. Available: https://www.hackmageddon.com/2020/05/26/16-30-april-2020-cyber-attacks-timeline/ [Accessed 30 July 2020].

178. Catalin Cimpanu, "Details of 20 Million Aptoide App Store Users Leaked on Hacking Forum," Zero Day, 17 April 2020. [Online]. Available: https://www.zdnet.com/article/details-of-20-million-aptoide-app-store-users-leaked-on-hacking-forum/ [Accessed 30 July 2020].

179. Catalin Cimpanu, "Nintendo Says 160,000 Users Impacted in Recent Account Hacks," Zero Day, 24 April 2020. [Online]. Available: https://www.zdnet.com/article/nintendo-says-160000-users-impacted-in-recent-account-hacks/ [Accessed 30 July 2020].

180. Jonathan Vanian, "Nintendo suffers major hack affecting 160,000 online accounts," Fortune, 24 April 2020. [Online]. Available: https://fortune.com/2020/04/24/nintendo-hack-switch-data-accounts/ [Accessed 30 July 2020].

181. Agence France-Presse, "Nintendo Says 300,000 Accounts Breached After Hack," The Jakarta Post, 10 June 2020. [Online]. Available: https://www.thejakartapost.com/life/2020/06/10/nintendo-says-300000-accounts-breached-after-hack.html [Accessed 30 July 2020].

182. Taylor Lyles, "Nintendo's NNID Hack Was Almost Twice as Big as First Reported," The Verge, 9 June 2020. [Online]. Available: https://www.theverge.com/2020/6/9/21285084/nintendo-nnid-switch-hack-accounts-affected-exposed [Accessed 30 July 2020].

183. Joe Tidy, "Twitter Hack: What went Wrong and Why It Matters," BBC News, 16 July 2020. [Online]. Available: https://www.bbc.com/news/technology-53428304 [Accessed 31 July 2020].

184. J. Agate and O. O'Rorke, "Data protection in media litigation," Communications Law, vol. 21, no. 2, p. 46–48, 2016.

185. J. V. DeMarco and B. A. Fox, "Data rights and data wrongs: Civil litigation and the new privacy norms," The Yale Law Journal, vol. 128, no. 2018–2019, 2019.

186. Open Data Watch, "DATA in the time of COVID-19," Open Data Watch, 27 July 2020. [Online]. Available: https://opendatawatch.com/what-is-being-said/data-in-the-time-of-covid-19/ [Accessed 31 July 2020].

187. Rositsa Zaimova, "How Data Can Help Fight a Health Crisis Like the Coronavirus," World Economic Forum, 31 March 2020. [Online]. Available: https://www.weforum.org/agenda/2020/03/role-data-fight-coronavirus-epidemic/ [Accessed 31 July 2020].

188. Sarah Coble, "Indonesia Denies #COVID19 Test Data Breach," Information Security Magazine, 22 June 2020. [Online]. Available: https://www.infosecurity-magazine.com/news/indonesia-denies-covid19-test-data/ [Accessed 31 July 2020].

189. Petir Garda Bhwana, "Ministry Still Tracing Indonesia's COVID-19 Patients Data Leak," Tempo, 21 June 2020. [Online]. Available: https://en.tempo.co/read/1356052/ministry-still-tracing-indonesias-covid-19-patients-data-leak [Accessed 31 July 2020].

190. Lucas Matney, "Twitter Stock Slides After-Hours amid Scramble to Contain High-profile Account Hacks," Tech Crunch, 15 July 2020. [Online]. Available: https://techcrunch.com/2020/07/15/twitter-stock-slides-after-hours-amid-scramble-to-contain-high-profile-account-hacks/ [Accessed 31 July 2020].

191. Reuters, "Twitter Shares Stumble after High-profile, Unprecedented Hack," Financial Express, 16 July 2020. [Online]. Available: https://www.financialexpress.com/market/twitter-shares-stumble-after-high-profile-unprecedented-hack/2026292/#:~:text=Shares%20of%20Twitter%20Inc%20dropped,%2C%20billionaires%2C%20celebrities%20and%20companies [Accessed 31 July 2020].

192. Shalini Nagarajan, "Twitter Stock Dives in Pre-market after a Widespread Hack Took Control of Major Celebrities' Accounts Including Bill Gates, Elon Musk, and Warren Buffett," Business Insider, 16 July 2020. [Online]. Available: https://markets.businessinsider.com/currencies/news/twitter-shares-down-7-pre-market-trading-after-bitcoin-hack-2020-7-1029400767# [Accessed 31 July 2020].

193. Associated Press, CNN, "Morning Headlines: Trump Demotes Campaign Chief; Twitter Hack Fallout; 'Magic School Bus' Author Dies," Madison, 16 July 2020. [Online]. Available: https://madison.com/news/national/morning-headlines-trump-demotes-campaign-chief-twitter-hack-fall-out-magic-school-bus-author-dies/article_95bb0929-f9e2-531b-a191-c7e2092350f5.html [Accessed 31 July 2020].

194. Colm Quinn, "An Insecure Twitter Means an Insecure World," Foreign Policy, 16 July 2020. [Online]. Available: https://foreignpolicy.com/2020/07/16/twitter-hack-insecure-world/ [Accessed 31 July 2020].

195. Al-Arshani S. and Samuelsohn D., "Trump Demotes Brad Parscale, Brings on Bill Stepien as New Campaign Manager," Business Insider Africa, 16 July 2020. [Online]. Available: https://africa.businessinsider.com/politics/trump-demotes-brad-parscale-brings-on-bill-stepien-as-new-campaign-manager/p6sd4xl [Accessed 31 July 2020].

196. J. Dawsey and M. Scherer, "Trump Replaces Campaign Manager as Polls Show Him Trailing Biden in Presidential Race," Washington Post, 16 July 2020. [Online]. Available: https://www.washingtonpost.com/politics/trump-parscale-stepien-campaign-manager/2020/07/15/91aad9b6-c6fd-11ea-8ffe-372be8d82298_story.html [Accessed 31 July 2020].

197. Federal Bureau of Investigation (FBI), "2019 Internet Crime Report," FBI Internet Crime Compliant Center, Washington D.C, 2020 https://pdf.ic3.gov/2019_IC3Report.pdf

198. Federal Bureau of Investigation (FBI), "2018 Internet Crime Report," FBI Internet Crime Compliant Center, Washington D.C, 2019 https://pdf.ic3.gov/2018_IC3Report.pdf

199. B. Johnson Derek, "Cyber Crime Cost Organizations $2.7 Billion in 2018," FWC, 19 April 2019. [Online]. Available: https://fcw.com/articles/2019/04/22/cyber-crime-stats.aspx [Accessed 1 August 2020].

200. "Top 6 Common Types of Cyberattacks in 2020," DNS Stuff, 12 May 2020. [Online]. Available: https://www.dnsstuff.com/common-types-of-cyber-attacks [Accessed 31 July 2020].

201. Eric Cole, "NSA Warns of Russian Attacks on Email Servers," Secure Anchor, 2 June 2020. [Online]. Available: https://www.secure-anchor.com/nsa-warns-of-russian-attacks-on-email-servers/?inf_contact_key=4e62686bd7e7cb7c3a5 19a678f990223b7af0999dac2af6212784c39e05d2aef [Accessed 9 June 2020].

Challenges of Managing Cybersecurity at COVID-19

5

The COVID-19 induced adjustments in the networked systems of organizations left them vulnerable to cyberattacks, and managing Cybersecurity incidents during the pandemic was challenging for several reasons.

Firstly, the nature of the spread of the virus imposed logistic limitations that initially inhibited the feasibility of a coordinated global Cybersecurity approach as each region resorted to self-help to cyber defense. Advisories on the anticipated Cybersecurity fallouts were either non-existent, lacked wide publicity, or were applied late when the cyberattacks had already gained momentum. It was as though cyber criminals were waiting to exploit the impending crisis. The initial impacts created more psychological apprehension and hampered attempts to evolve a global scale emergency data protection strategy.

The fear of contracting the disease was so captivating that Cybersecurity vendors struggled to balance the medical safety of their workforce against the urgency of developing solutions to protect the cyberspace. Amid the panic over rising infection figures, personnel needed time to settle down, self-isolate, adapt to the lockdown restrictions, stockpile food, and think clearly under such unfamiliar conditions. That timeframe to settle down was cleverly exploited by cyber criminals in a typical zero-day style as if it was an opportunity being awaited and prepared for, long before.

Secondly, many potential targets succumbed easily to social engineering threats due to the panic which made every online resource purportedly linked to coronavirus disease to appear attractive including deceptive web portals and email scams that stylishly embedded malware. The human vulnerability angle, exhibited out of shear desperation, made a nonsense of subsisting social engineering ethics. People just wanted to remain alive, and so any online resource that had a semblance of coronavirus update, cure, vaccine [1], therapy, solution, recovery, and like terms became enticing and irresistibly clickable. As a result, cyber criminals took advantage of people's desperation and fear to propagate malware [2].

Thirdly, each good-intentioned global response to the COVID-19 pandemic was in some way exploited by malicious hackers to initiate a unique type of attack, and this created risks of data loss, identity theft, and operational disruption. Table 4.1 matches various COVID-19 interventions with the corresponding Cybersecurity risks associated with them and highlights how hackers and online fraudsters took advantage of genuine measures intended to curb the spread of the virus at the time.

5.1 IDENTITY AND ACCESS CONTROL CHALLENGES

5.1.1 Authentication Challenges

Authentication is the confirmation of a person against a pre-established identity for the sake of accessing a service [3]. It is the process of verifying the genuineness of an identity as a condition for granting user access into an information system. Poorly protected user access can become an attacker's entry point into a target system [4]. COVID-19 witnessed an amplification of the issues inherent in existing authentication protocols, especially those that deal with remote access and encryption. High profile breaches occurred due to authentication breakdown.

The inability to undertake proper authentication is a key driver of cybercrime, leaving digital identities vulnerable to exploitation by malicious hackers. It also impacts on the confidentiality, integrity, and availability of the data of other legitimate users and is linked to identity theft related abuses such as spear phishing, spamming, cyber espionage, and ransomware, and other disruptive threats including man-in-the-middle attack and distributed denial of service.

5.1.2 Authorization Challenges

Authorization challenges refer to issues with the process of assigning roles and privileges to a verified user. In this regard, the challenges surrounding the extent to which COVID-19 influenced the security of authorization techniques are significant.

5.1.3 Accountability Challenges

In access control, accountability means the ability to keep chronological and transactional track of digital activities of an authenticated user on any digital resource whether online, offline, or local. Poor accountability owing to COVID-19 adjustments on many ocassions narrowed tracking capabilities and restricted the audit of digital footprints, which ultimately created trust issues.

5.2 INCIDENT MANAGEMENT CHALLENGES

As organizations and individuals were preoccupied with strategies for staying alive and safe from COVID-19, incident management became severely challenged for most organizations whose workforce had suddenly depleted physically due to the lockdown, or whose full network defenses had become impacted by the remote work adoption. In both instances, the tradeoffs worked against incident response and incident handling.

5.2.1 Incident Response Challenges

Due to the peculiarities of the moment, most organizations suddenly lacked the full capacity to initiate and observe the full cycle of computer incident response, especially identification, containment, eradication, and recovery. The psychological balance to undertake procedural response was in conflict with the anxiety of staying safe from contracting the virus.

5.2.2 Incident Handling Challenges

The problems associated with the management of COVID-19-related cyber incidents were centered around lawful disclosures to law enforcement and ethical reporting to regulatory bodies. A lot of organizations were reluctant to report cyber breaches in which they were directly involved or affected, for fear of media backlash and to evade regulatory sanctions. For such organizations, speculative leaks became the alternative with their attendant repercussions including misrepresentation of facts due to unconventional reporting.

5.3 REMOTE COMMUNICATIONS CHALLENGES

5.3.1 Work from Home Challenges

COVID-19 saw an unprecedented adoption of telecommuting and video conferencing [5] as innovative alternatives for remote work and office productivity, colloquially referred to as teleworking, mobile working, home working, or work from home (WFH) [6]. As many technology vendors modified relevant portions of their product and service offerings to reflect the booming global adoption of WFH, organizations refined their remote work policies to accommodate the new realities.

Similarly, government agencies, corporate institutions, and healthcare delivery organizations developed strategies to ensure adequate protection for employees, business associates, and healthcare workers, respectively [7].

While some companies had strict security controls for remote privileged access, many others did not [8], and these conflicting disparities threw up fresh challenges during the crises. The new craze was the WFH concept as millions of businesses struggled to contend with the option of managing a completely remote workforce with the aid of telecommuting and related technologies.

Although the Cybersecurity risks arising from vulnerabilities in remote technologies were not particularly new, the social distancing protocols in the pandemic compounded the crisis by compelling employees to work more from home or remote locations. Consequently, as people sought new ways to stay connected, malicious hackers also took advantage of the attitudinal changes in the online workplace, and launched large-scale cyber exploits against vulnerable targets. The following challenges were very rampant with the WFH concept and applications during the pandemic:

- *Unpreparedness*

  Many organizations were totally unprepared for, and undecided on actions [9]. This initial confusion was good news to hackers who capitalized on the anxiety and indecision to penetrate vulnerable networks through cyber espionage, man-in-the-middle attack, and denial of access.

- *Resistance to change*

  Employee mindset and resistance to change were overwhelming. Those who were used to working from a home office prior to the pandemic as an integral part of work flexibility, and already conversant with using telecommuting applications for remote connections and client interactions, adjusted faster to the COVID-19 WFH shift than others [5]. For such people, the shift was less of a change.

  However, those whom it was new to, experienced a transitory period of adjustment during which initial resistance and conflicts occurred, compounded by some levels of isolation and loneliness.

- *Unsafe networks*

  Poor network conditions and inadequate bandwidth were two major network-related issues that challenged remote communication technology during the pandemic, and these were mostly from carry-over hiccups in the technology of use.

  Up to the early 2000s, the legacy internet telephony systems were characterized by high latency, jitters, and echoes on Sipura, Media ring, Delta3, Net2phone, and other early VOIP platforms [10]. With progressive research by the Internet Engineering Task Force (IETF), the Institute of Electrical and Electronic Engineers (IEEE), and vendor markets, contemporary solutions have surmounted these initial hiccups. However, design concepts and environments of use remain sources of technical concern for unsafe networks.

  Unsafe networks comprising of channels that were unregulated, poorly-protected, or unencrypted constituted a major weakness which hackers preyed on to launch cyberattacks that diminished or disrupted the quality of the telecommuting session. The porosity of insecure networks was easily spotted by hackers during pre-attack reconnaissance to discover exploitable loopholes including unencrypted channels, factory default device login credentials, weak authentication protocols, outdated devices drivers, unpatched software, and obsolete operating systems.

- *Distraction errors*

  The distraction of combining WFH with leisure and domestic chores increased the risks of thoughtlessly introducing malware links into the company's computer network and exposing employers and colleagues to cyberattacks through business email compromise or related services. Many remote workers fell victims to distraction errors including wrong entries, obscene backgrounds, and delayed responses during online sessions.

Other remote communication challenges [5] included the following:

- Capacity gap with ignorant employees.
- Data security ethical issues.
- Insecure communication terminals.
- Insider collusion.
- Social engineering threats.

Remote working conditions left many businesses vulnerable to cybercrime [11], and the high tech sector was often ground zero for cyberattacks. One possible explanation is that these organizations, either own, and control systems that process other people's valuable data, or offer vital services that have the potential to reach out and impact more people quicker and easier, e.g., healthcare device manufacturing and e-commerce application development. Both conditions (i.e., data control and expansive coverage) are the typical key attractions to hackers and internet fraudsters whose end goals remain fame, illicit financial gains, and propagation of political ideologies.

5.3.2 Telecommuting and Video Conferencing Challenges

Communicating over a distance via high speed networks received an upsurge of patronage as a result of the COVID-19 lockdown measures. Unfortunately, the popularity of telecommuting and video conferencing applications also opened up potential avenues for hostile hacking incidents that targeted porous networks and unsafe systems and applications, thereby raising serious concerns over data safety, privacy protection, and online ethics.

5.4 HEALTHCARE DATA MANAGEMENT CHALLENGES

Security in the healthcare industry is crucial as it involves patients' personal information and private medical details [12]. Besides, the industry is built on peoples' trust, and any breach may result in unfavourable consequences. It was truly challenging managing healthcare data within the industry at the time of the pandemic, especially during the lockdown.

The healthcare industry was the epicentre of cybercrimes during the pandemic. As one of the world's biggest and widest developing industries [13], it is also one of the most vulnerable in terms of Cybersecurity [12] by virtue of the sensitive nature of healthcare data which make it both valuable and attractive to cyber criminals. As a result, hackers would capitalize on poorly-protected systems to steal confidential medical information, manipulate health insurance data, and disrupt operations involving patient's diagnosis information.

Ransomware attacks were targeted at facilities treating COVID-19 patients, testing potential vaccines, and distributing PPEs, a situation that further complicated efforts to ensure public health and safety [14]. These facilities were attractive targets for cyber criminals as their services were vital to the crisis, which also implied an increased likelihood to pay ransom if impacted.

Healthcare data is a collection of information about the health status or medical condition of an individual, or statistical data relating to the well-being of a group managed under a single therapeutic control. It provides critical information about a patient, and becomes even more delicate to handle when it is in electronic form, providing life-saving information in an Electronic Health Record (EHR).

5.4.1 Value-Based Classification of Healthcare Data

Value-based classification associates healthcare data with Personally Identifiable Information (PII) and Protected Health Information (PHI), two components that represent valuable information about the health status of a patient. They both require special protection to prevent unauthorized access and illegal modification, both of which have severe medical impacts on healthcare beneficiaries.

While a PII defines a person's identity and can distinguish one person from another, a PHI is any set of information relating to healthcare, medical conditions, or clinical records collected of a person for the purpose of administering healthcare and monitoring health status [15]. PHI includes health records, health histories, laboratory test results, and medical bills that provide an identity for potential patients to determine appropriate levels of healthcare. Owing to their sensitive nature, both PIIs and PHIs require superior security to prevent heavy consequences that could arise from their compromise.

A patient's diagnosis report is a personal information about the outcome of a medical examination, poor management of which could lead to stigmatization and misdiagnosis. Misinformation through altered medical reports can lead to patient trauma [16]. As a result, such sensitive information requires strict privacy protection. Figure 5.1 gives an illustration of PHIs recognized by the Health Insurance Portability and Accountability Act (HIPAA) that require proper protection at all times. HIPAA rules limit the use and disclosure of PHIs [17].

Table 5.1 shows a listing of sensitive healthcare data alongside the Cybersecurity protection they require.

Generally, people expected to access healthcare as quickly as they fell sick, they also wanted effective referral and billing using accurate and reliable health data [15]. As a result of the urgent need for accurate health data, Cybersecurity [2] was at the front burner to perform its three most critical functions:

- Systematically **prevent** cyberattacks and security breaches targeting vulnerable health data and information systems.
- Proactively **detect** planned cyberattacks and network intrusions against health data.
- Promptly **respond** to active cyberattacks and advanced threats and minimize their impact.

The Cybersecurity dimension of managing healthcare data in the COVID-19 era relied heavily on the classification of health data [13, 18] based on value, sensitivity and privacy, as well as its criticality to life, well-being, and as life-saving information.

5.4.2 Confidentiality Challenges

Loss of confidentiality occurs when information or data is exposed to unauthorized persons, or released prematurely ahead of its time of use or disclosure. Announcing a patient's health condition on social media is unprofessional, unethical, and violates the confidentiality principle. Threats to healthcare data confidentiality during the pandemic included the following:

- Unauthorized access or knowledge of personal health record.
- Unauthorized disclosure of sensitive health information.
- Illegal view of patient's health profile or healthcare identity.
- Illegal knowledge of patient's medical condition.

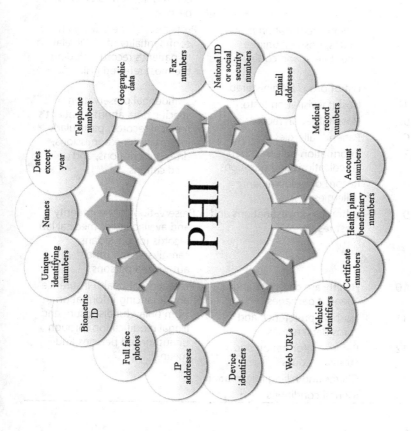

FIGURE 5.1 Protected Health Information (PHI) identifiers.

TABLE 5.1   Cybersecurity protection required for various healthcare data

S NO.	HEALTHCARE DATA TYPE	SCOPE OF CYBERSECURITY PROTECTION
1.	Patient's name, medical diagnosis, disease treatment, and health status	Protection of medical records from unauthorized disclosure, illegal access, and unethical communication to external parties.
2.	Patient's registration profile, dates, hospital unique identifiers, and codes	Protection of the privacy and confidentiality of all PII relating to patient's record including the most referred PHI.
3.	List of drugs administered	Confidential preservation of specific data about a patient's medical records, particularly information on admissions, drug prescriptions, and medications.
4.	Hospital visitation history	
5.	Hospitalization record	
6.	Patient's allergies	
7.	Information on prescribed medications and durations	
8.	Record of predominant allergies	
9.	Laboratory investigations and test results	Preservation of the integrity and availability of medical lab records for physicians, caregivers, and other authorized persons.
10.	Healthcare coverage and benefit packages	Protection of health insurance and financing information from unlawful disclosure and illegal modification through unauthorized persons and means.
11.	Hospital preference and providers' names	
12.	Referral information and transfer codes	
13.	Claims and billing information	
14.	Mental conditions	

5.4.3 Integrity Challenges

Healthcare data is said to have lost its integrity when it is modified by unauthorized means or persons, or under illegal circumstances. Deletion of healthcare data by unauthorized persons compromises its integrity and places the original data owner at risk of misdiagnosis and medical

TABLE 5.2   Description of unauthorized modifications of healthcare data

S. NO.	VARIANT	DESCRIPTION
1.	Data addition	Unauthorized inclusion of an item that was not originally part of the healthcare data. This is also called data padding.
2.	Data subtraction	Unauthorized removal of a part of data item that was meant to be part of the complete healthcare data.
3.	Data substitution	Unauthorized replacement of a health record with another from an external source.
4.	Data relocation	Movement of healthcare data to a new unintended or unapproved location.
5.	Data swapping	Switching the positions of two or more healthcare data items, one in place of each other.
6.	Data deletion	Total removal of specific items from the healthcare data of a living or dead person.
7.	Record deletion	Removal of the entire health record of a specific living or dead person.
8.	Data masking	Placing a deceptive or misleading label on data to give it a falsified meaning or manipulated interpretation. It is any form of distortion to the originality of data identity.
9.	Data pseudonymization	Masking data with a name or label that is unrelated to its content and that does not represent its content, e.g., nicknames or aliases.
10.	Data anonymization	Deliberately making the origin, location, or identity of data unknown, hidden, or concealing its identity.

emergencies. Table 5.2 shows some variants of unauthorized modification of healthcare data.

Integrity-based threats to healthcare data during the pandemic included the following:

- Loss of patient's data or medical record to disaster.
- Theft of health record of a patient.
- Unauthorized modification of healthcare data.
- Accidental deletion of health information.

- Malicious deletion of part of or whole record of a patient's medical history.
- Unplanned or unauthorized duplication of healthcare data.

5.4.4 Availability Challenges

Health information is said to have lost its availability when it proves difficult to access in a timely manner or when it is completely inaccessible due to system failure, virus, ransomware, a cyber breach, power hiccup, network fault, sabotage, etc.

COVID-19 lockdown protocols caused peculiar limitations that led to delays in accessing healthcare by patients, and disruption of medical operations in some cases.

There were instances of medical records and health information trapped within systems that were compromised by ransomware to the extent of patients being denied healthcare on account of missing or inaccessible patients' records. In most cases, such inaccessibility was traced to inadequate data disposal methods which exposed sensitive PHI to different hacker activities including eavesdropping, recycling, and brute recovery. Standard disposal techniques were impacted by the social distancing protocols that had become the new normal.

The availability-based threats to healthcare data that dominated the pandemic included:

- System shutdown.
- Unfavourable environmental control system.
- Network delays.
- Website hijack.
- Internet slowness and unstable network resources.
- Database hacking.
- Locked accounts.
- Power supply fluctuations.

As the pandemic raged, the need for timely, accurate, and real-time health data continued to rise [15]. Table 5.3 summarizes the most critical beneficiaries of healthcare data during the crises.

TABLE 5.3 The need for health data and medical statistics during the pandemic

S. NO.	ENTITY	JUSTIFICATION FOR NEED OF HEALTHCARE DATA
1.	Hospitals and medical centres	Real-time data on COVID-19 hospitalization, recoveries, referrals, emergency cases, and fatality figures.
2.	Governments and health regulatory authorities	Data for budgetary purposes, and for monitoring the purchase and distribution of medical facilities for management of COVID-19 cases including ventilators, PPEs, test kits, etc.
3.	Radiologists and medical laboratory personnel	Data for coordinating COVID-19 testing logistics at laboratories, and for appraising the efficacy of test kits.
4.	Clinicians and frontline medical workers	Healthcare data for disease mapping and decision-making on confirmed infected patients in designated COVID-19 treatment facilities.
5.	Pharmaceutical companies	Data for planning the production, market segmentation, and prioritized distribution of drugs for the treatment of COVID-19.
6.	Research institutes	Data providing feedback on health statistical records to strategize on drug analysis, particularly clinical analysis of vaccine trials, and future operations.
7.	Epidemiologists	Firsthand information and reliable data for managing confirmed cases in hospital quarantine facilities as well as suspected contacts in isolation centres.
8.	Medical statisticians	Reliable data for performing unbiased analysis of disease prevalence in real-time for the purpose of releasing reliable analytics for global consumption.
9.	Health insurance companies	Accurate data for managing healthcare financing, coordinating referrals, and for promptly computing error-free insurance claims for their beneficiaries.
10.	Health funders and philanthropic organizations	Trustworthy information to guide the focus of their investments [1] and medical funding, and mobilization of additional resources based on areas of pressing need such as shortage of medical supplies and PPEs.

Source:
[1] World Health Organization, "COVID 19 Public Health Emergency of International Concern (PHEIC) Global Research and Innovation Forum: *Towards a research roadmap,*" *World Health Organization R&D Blueprint: Global Research Collaboration for Infectious Disease Preparedness.*, Geneva, 2020.

5.5 CHAPTER SUMMARY

COVID-19 became a major catalyst for growing cyberattacks as employees working from home did not have access to the same enterprise-level security architectures in their workplace [19]. This challenge, in addition to the initial uncertainties associated with the pandemic, increased online vulnerabilities and ignited a wave of cyberattacks that exploited vulnerable systems, using email phishing, social engineering, and other techniques.

Managing Cybersecurity became grossly challenged as cyber criminals took advantage of human fear and apprehension to distribute destructive malware codes concealed as authentic coronavirus information and stole confidential information in the process [2]. Besides, most attacks used social engineering as their entry point, and this made it even harder to detect and mitigate, particularly in the management of healthcare data. It is a required Cybersecurity practice to ensure access to reliable healthcare data whenever required by beneficiaries.

Many of the identified challenges bothered on access control as users undertook unsafe actions that were panic-induced and totally against all known authentication best practices such as choosing weak passwords, and relaxing audit trail processes. In majority of the cyberattack episodes, proactive incident response was either lacking or inactive, and this further exposed confidential healthcare data to threat of privacy infringements, particularly in medical facilities where pressure on medical supplies mounted.

REFERENCES

1. R. Zhang, Y. Li, A. L. Zhang, Y. Wang and M. J. Molina, "Identifying airborne transmission as the dominant route for the spread of COVID-19," *Proceedings of the National Academy of Sciences (PNAS) of the United States of America,* vol. 117, no. 26, pp. 14857–14863, 2020.

2. K. U. Okereafor and O. Adebola, "Tackling the cybersecurity impacts of the coronavirus outbreak as a challenge to internet safety," *International Journal in IT and Engineering (IJITE)*, vol. 8, no. 2, pp. 1–14, 2020.
3. P. Makin and C. M. Meier, "6 Things You May Not Know About Biometrics," CGAP, 26 July 2018. [Online]. Available: https://www.cgap.org/blog/6-things-you-may-not-know-about-biometrics [Accessed 23 May 2020].
4. Z. A. Wen, Z. Lin, R. Chen and E. Andersen, "What. hack: Engaging anti-phishing training through a role-playing phishing simulation game," in *2019 CHI Conference on Human Factors in Computing Systems*, Glasgow, Scotland, 2019.
5. K. Okereafor and P. Manny, "Understanding cybersecurity challenges of telecommuting and video conferencing applications in the COVID-19 pandemic," *International Journal in IT & Engineering*, vol. 8, no. 6, pp. 13–23, 2020.
6. K. Okereafor and P. Manny, "Solving cybersecurity challenges of telecommuting and video conferencing applications in the COVID-19 pandemic," *International Journal in IT & Engineering (IJITE)*, vol. 8, no. 6, pp. 24–32, 2020.
7. K. A. Moore, M. Lipsitch, J. M. Barry and M. T. Osterholm, "COVID-19: The CIDRAP Viewpoint. Part 1: The Future of the COVID-19 Pandemic: Lessons Learned from Pandemic Influenza," Center for Infectious Disease Research and Policy (CIDRP), University of Minnesota, Minnesota, 2020.
8. J. Carson, "The Twitter Hack and the Failure to Protect Privileged Access," Thycotic, 17 July 2020. [Online]. Available: https://thycotic.com/company/blog/2020/07/17/twitter-hack-and-failure-to-protect-privileged-access/ [Accessed 21 July 2020].
9. M. Phil, "CISO Alliance Nigeria (Lagos & Abuja) Virtual Catch Up/Covid 19 Update April 7th 2020," Alliance Media Group, Lagos, 2020.
10. Y. Fayyaz, D. M. Khan and F. Fayyaz, "The evaluation of voice-over internet protocol (VoIP) by means of trixbox," *International Journal of Natural and Engineering Sciences*, vol. 10, no. 3, pp. 33–41, 2016.
11. Deloitte, "Global cyber executive briefing. High technology," Deloitte, London, 2015.
12. S. Alexandra, "Cybersecurity & Healthcare during COVID-19," GlobalSign, 13 April 2020. [Online]. Available: https://www.globalsign.com/en/blog/cyber-security-healthcare-during-covid-19 [Accessed 5 August 2020].
13. B. K. Rai, "Big data in healthcare management: A review of literature," *American Journal of Theoretical and Applied Business*, vol. 4, no. 2, pp. 57–69, 2018.
14. NJCCIC Advisory, "Cyber Threats & Cybersecurity for Healthcare during COVID-19," New Jersey Cybersecurity and Communications Integration Cell (NJCCIC), 8 April 2020. [Online]. Available: https://www.cyber.nj.gov/alerts-advisories/cyber-threats-cybersecurity-for-healthcare-during-covid-19 [Accessed 5 August 2020].
15. K. Okereafor and A. Marcelo, "Addressing cybersecurity challenges of health data in the COVID-19 pandemic," *International Journal in IT & Engineering*, vol. 8, no. 6, pp. 1–12, 2020.

16. S. Blog, "5 Cybersecurity Threats of 2020," Soliton, 20 May 2020. [Online]. Available: https://solitonsys.com/blog/5-cybersecurity-threats-of-2020/ [Accessed 30 July 2020].

17. S. Alder, "What is considered PHI under HIPAA?" HIPAA Journal, Dublin, Ireland, 2017.

18. Z. Ansari, Q. H. Mateenuddin and A. Abdullah, "Performance research on medical data classification using traditional and soft computing techniques," *International Journal of Recent Technology and Engineering (IJRTE)*, vol. 8, no. 2S3, pp. 990–995, 2019.

19. M. M. Shivanandhan, "10 Tools You Should Know as a Cybersecurity Engineer," FreeCodeCamp, 6 August 2020. [Online]. Available: https://www-freecodecamp-org.cdn.ampproject.org/v/s/www.freecodecamp.org/news/10-tools-you-should-know-as-a-cybersecurity-engineer/amp/?usqp=mq331A QFKAGwASA%3D&amp_js_v=0.1#referrer=https%3A%2F%2Fwww.google.com&amp_tf=From%20%251%24s&ampshare=https%3A%2F% [Accessed 8 August 2020].

Cyberattack Mitigations During the Pandemic

6

The nature and frequency of Cybersecurity incidents during the COVID-19 pandemic required an approach that would provide multiple layers of protection for digital assets and yet offer performance with minimal service disruptions. Given their scope and sophistication, only a defense in-depth model could have sufficiently tackled their unpredictability.

A defense in-depth Cybersecurity model is the simultaneous application of several control measures to a single-valued asset to optimize efficacy. The control measures make up the defense in-depth approach work in a complementary manner, ensuring that at any time the asset is safeguarded by two or more layers of protection for maximum security.

6.1 SCENARIO OF DEFENSE IN-DEPTH

An authentication server for national electronic identity database hosted on a *remote virtual machine* that is situated behind *three hardware-based firewalls* on daisy chain redundancy, inside a *biometrically secured data centre* that is fitted with *environmental control systems* and *fire management solutions* and linked to *three internet-facing networks*, in addition to being manned by *shift duty armed guards* who routinely receive *security briefing* and undergo *scheduled fire drills* at the *muster point* every three days.

The italicized keywords and terms in the scenario above are used to illustrate each of the three Cybersecurity countermeasures in Table 6.1.

TABLE 6.1   Defense in-depth Cybersecurity mitigation approach using sample scenario

SN	MITIGATION	CONCEPT APPLIED	COUNTERMEASURE	GUARANTEE
1.	Remote hosting	Disaster recovery	Administrative	Availability
2.	Virtual machine	Redundancy	Technical	Availability
3.	Multiple firewalls	Redundancy	Technical	Availability
4.	Biometrically secured	Secure authentication	Technical	Confidentiality, integrity, availability
5.	Data centre	Environmental safety for equipment	Physical	Integrity, availability
6.	Environmental control system		Physical	Integrity, availability
7.	Fire management solutions		Physical	Integrity, availability
8.	Three internet facing networks	Multi-homed connectivity	Technical	Availability
9.	Encrypted	Encryption	Technical	Confidentiality, integrity
10.	Shift duty	Job rotation	Administrative	Confidentiality, integrity, availability
11.	Armed guards	Access control	Physical	Integrity, availability
12.	Security briefing	Cybersecurity awareness and training policy	Administrative	Confidentiality, integrity, availability
13.	Scheduled		Administrative	Confidentiality, integrity, availability
14.	Fire drills		Administrative	
15.	Muster point	Environmental safety for personnel	Administrative	

6.2 ADMINISTRATIVE COUNTERMEASURES

Policies and technical guidelines have become a critical countermeasure for several reasons. Apart from guiding standardization of Cybersecurity interventions, they also keep track of behavioural adjustments of digital consumers in response to the dynamics of the cyberspace such as the digital upsurge occasioned by the COVID-19 pandemic.

Corporate organizations and other entities found solace in complying with online Cybersecurity guidelines but were uncertain of the origin and authenticity of guidelines in fear of falling prey to orchestrated online scams. In addressing the issues, and as early warning notices went round, organizations with such responsibilities struggled to issue directives as appropriate. At some point, the World Health Organization Academy released a mobile App to aid people in seeking COVID-19 information. The App which was available for both Android and iOS devices automated the steps for searching for and obtaining authentic COVID-19 information and statistics from a trustworthy platform.

6.3 PHYSICAL COUNTERMEASURES

Physical countermeasures are security controls that rely on tangible interventions to protect assets. Whether they are CCTV surveillance systems for monitoring restricted areas such as a Tier-3 data centre or armed security personnel who guard against intruders using mantraps, physical countermeasures provide security at the operational level and include the following: biometric time and attendance machine, sniffers dog, perimeter fencing, employee badge, muster point, fire suppressor, motion detector, CCTV, environmental control system, raised floor, cable tray, etc.

6.4 TECHNICAL COUNTERMEASURES

Technical countermeasures represent the tangible security assets used to protect data networks or computer resources against various types of compromise or to minimize the impacts of real attacks. They include software and hardware systems that perform preventive, detective, reactive functions such as anti-virus software, network monitoring tool, encryption software, etc.

Encryption is an aspect of technical countermeasure used to protect documents being exchanged across parties to ensure data integrity and user identification. COVID-19 saw an increasing amount of transactions being sealed online using such technologies to endorse documents for real estate, publishing contracts, purchase orders, consent transfer, etc. For example, the DocuSign tool enables parties to use electronic signatures remotely for endorsing contractual agreements on a variety of devices.

6.5 CONTROL KNOBS

Categorizing security countermeasures by respective safety controls balance their effectiveness in line with the defense in-depth model. Control knobs are safety measures implemented to manage threats and security risks targeting vulnerable computer systems and networks. Five control knobs are reviewed.

6.5.1 Preventive Control

Preventive control systems protect digital assets (including data) from known and unknown threats, either by minimizing the risk, reducing the exposure, or halting the progression of the threat. These measures are designed to prevent errors, inaccuracies, irregularities, or fraud from occurring in the first place. They also help to avert data loss and guarantee online safety by ensuring confidentiality, integrity, and availability.

6.5.1.1 Zoom preventive intervention

In the peak of the pandemic when countries had closed their borders in compliance with the lockdown protocols, and when it became obvious that remote technologies would be handy alternatives for corporate meetings and work interactions, Zoom, the online video telephony company optimized its *waiting room* feature allowing a virtual meeting administrator to carry out pre-screening of meeting participants before admitting them into a live video conferencing session.

Zoom's *waiting room* functionality represents a typical preventive control knob that pre-checks potential meeting participants and minimizes the risk of zoom-bombing where an intruder uses the man-in-the-middle attack to intercept and/or record meeting conversations. This neutralizes the intruvder's efforts to sneak in undetected to capture sensitive information or post offensive content that could harm reputation and privacy trigger.

6.5.1.2 Anti-malware preventive intervention

Of significance to the pandemic period was the installation of an effective anti-malware tool such as antivirus software designed to identify contents that are potentially harmful to the computer, particularly those disguised as coronavirus resources. Having a functional anti-malware tool on internet-connected devices turned out to be a profitable approach for users that embraced it.

A good antivirus or anti-malware solution can apply an advanced detection mechanism to detect the most common strings of malicious codes and can take actions to protect systems and data. Prior to choosing and installing an antivirus tool, users would expectedly ascertain performance features, confirm available support by the antivirus software providers, as well as keep the antivirus software fully updated for maximum efficiency.

6.5.2 Detective Control

Detective controls are typically intended to uncover the existence of errors, inaccuracies, or fraud that have already occurred.

6.5.3 Responsive Control

Responsive controls are reactive countermeasures, required after a breach. They are designed to uncover the root cause, facilitate faster recovery, limit overall impact, and forestall spread.

6.5.4 Corrective Control

Corrective controls complement responsive countermeasures to fix what has been compromised by a cyber breach, by triggering recovery and retrieval actions.

6.5.5 Deterrent Control

Deterrent countermeasures are intended to discourage the attacker by prolonging the attack with the hope that by making the attack more difficult, the adversary could give up on the efforts. E.g. the use of a strong password is intended to elongate the time it takes for the malicious hacker to crack using brute force or dictionary attack.

6.6 CHAPTER SUMMARY

As with all security incidents, the combination of administrative, physical, and technical countermeasures was in high expectations during the COVID-19 pandemic. They were expedient for the achievement of safer cyberspace.

Notwithstanding the strength of security deployed to detect and prevent cyberattacks that masqueraded as candid online coronavirus information, it was important for digital users to have a plan for recovery from active cyber breaches and mitigate their impacts. Essentially, recovery was to mimic the defense in-depth approach comprising of a combination of preventive, detective, responsive, corrective, and deterrent control knobs.

Cybersecurity in Post COVID-19 Digital Era

7

The period 2021 to 2025 will be characterized by fascinating Cybersecurity research and innovations that will optimize the sophistication of digital security tools, drawing lessons from the trend of COVID-19 related cyberattacks.

Although pandemics usually lead to changes in societal behaviour or in corporate mindset, the strong influence of COVID-19 on the Cybersecurity domain is projected to impact both. As the battle for supremacy between the cyberattackers and the cyber defenders continues, there is an expectation that post COVID-19 the digital world would transform both offensive and defensive tools with the increasing sophistication. The dynamics of this transformation has been stimulated by the nature of cyber breaches that dominated the period.

Behavioural changes are predicted in the optimization of cyberspace etiquettes, practices, and standards. Such changes are projected to ignite revision of some security standards on remote communications, online data transmission protocols, and the email system. It is also forecasted that some pre-existing Cybersecurity laws would undergo repeal. It is inevitable to see moves for the enactment of brand-new data protection guidelines for secure management of data life cycle particularly suitable for such major disruptive events comparable to the magnitude of the COVID-19 crisis.

In terms of corporate mindset, the reorientation of digital consumers through aggressive Cybersecurity awareness is a challenge, which the ICT industry could optimize to ramp up capabilities in all aspects of global computing. Thanks to the United Nation's establishment of the norms of responsible state behaviour in the cyberspace [1–5].

7.1 CYBERSECURITY PROJECTIONS AFTER THE PANDEMIC

With COVID-19, more of our personal lives and business activities are being conducted online than ever [6]. As more employees continue to work remotely, with less protection due to remote access, the cyberspace continues to witness increasing number of sophisticated cyberattacks, with each attack appearing more unique and complex than the preceding one, and resulting in huge business losses [7]. Yet, the existing approaches to securing IT infrastructure are proving unreliable [8] and insufficient. Besides, there is a steady increase in the number of organizations that are pushing corporate data to the cloud despite unsafe and questionable security guarantees. For these reasons, future cyberattacks are projected to be not only more frequent but also much more dangerous [9], hence justifying the need for optimized alternatives to online safety. The period 2021 to 2025 will be characterized by fascinating Cybersecurity research and innovations that will optimize the sophistication of digital security tools and applications to the advantage of global business technologies.

Digital security and online safety can no longer be trivialized by organizations as an afterthought, given the rapidly evolving digital landscape amid the prevalence of sophisticated cyberattacks. The concerns on the influence of data security on global business technologies and how cyberattacks impact organizations and individuals, all together shape an enticing future for post-pandemic Cybersecurity.

Considering all the lessons, post-COVID-19 digital era looks exciting for global business technologies [10] in all of its components: computers, software applications, networking, cloud computing, telephone communications, accounting systems, customer relationship management systems, electronic document management system, business email communications, etc.

The momentum will be driven by predictive analytics of data from diverse sources across several complex intertwined systems. There is a huge Cybersecurity opportunity in data protection, as the pandemic's digital lessons trigger ground-breaking research and innovations in data management.

Lessons will also cause a fusion of precision technologies and predictive systems with artificial intelligence, big data (BD), telemedicine, and aviation data to form the next big thing (NBT).

7.1.1 Cybersecurity in Artificial Intelligence (AI)

As opposed to reactive and threat-centric security [11] that only mitigates damage after events occur, post COVID-19 Cybersecurity will prevent them from happening in the first place. The driving force of post COVID-19 Cybersecurity will be a fusion of machine learning with an expanded IoT framework that will incorporate BD analytics to power the next generation of cyber defense systems capable of advancing the frontiers of digital security beyond the physical realm.

As pre COVID-19 Cybersecurity has proven to be ineffective at stopping increasingly sophisticated external adversaries and insider threats, the evolution of the envisaged complex fusion of machine learning and BD will result in the systems whose multiple parts will require sophisticated security defenses to be driven purely by predictive analytics, the backbone of AI, in terms of predictive threat hunting, adaptive security mitigations, AI-driven event log and alert systems, and self-healing intelligent networks. With AI, the Cybersecurity possibilities are totally limitless.

With AI, there will be less emphasis on behaviour-based Cybersecurity systems, instead the focus will shift to complex systems that can better safeguard data and anticipate data loss incidents before they occur. Therefore, the next generation Cybersecurity in Artificial Intelligence will close the gap between human interpretation of security alerts and machine-oriented detect-and-respond capabilities, which will leave no room for human errors that are prevalent in today's defective Cybersecurity paradigms.

Proactive, predictive, and dynamic Cybersecurity in the post-pandemic era will use a combination of human behaviour analysis, modelling of risk scenarios, and applied AI [6] to narrowly focus on the entities that truly pose the highest levels of risk to a business and its employees [11] and be able to extract precise details to facilitate proactive action in the midst of machines that are capable of protecting themselves [8]. The precision of smarter next generation Cybersecurity in AI will be near perfection, leveraging the dexterity exhibited by some of the coordinated cybercrime incidents of the pandemic. An optimized Cybersecurity paradigm that gives more trustworthy cyberspace guarantee based on the automated contextual analysis of behaviour information is possible, and AI is the key to its actualization.

For example, an AI-enabled Cybersecurity using automatic speaker recognition technology could be optimized to match a voice to a person [12] for investigating high-profile cybercrime incidents involving telecommunications fraud, drug trafficking, kidnapping, and cyber espionage. This could also be applied for counterterrorism and predictive analytics of pre-ransomware attack stages by using neural networks to design software algorithms that listen to the isolated keywords in voice patterns and are able to predict suspected malicious plans with high-precision assurances.

According to International Data Corporation (IDC)'s prediction [13], by 2025, up to 49% of the world's stored data will reside in public cloud environments. This projection has a huge Cybersecurity connotation in terms of data safety and preparedness for the dynamism of corporate data in the cyberspace. An AI-driven Cybersecurity is most suitable for matching the dynamism of corporate data into the cloud and other forms of virtual presence, a trend that is on a steady increase. The fusion of AI into the next generation Cybersecurity could potentially generate results that can predict and avert devastating events by simply aggregating and analyzing indicators from multiple sources. With this envisaged reality, the predictability of future pandemics, even beyond the magnitude of COVID-19, will be a completely theoretical possibility.

7.1.2 Cybersecurity in Big Data

Societies and processes generate tons of BD and information from several sources, in multiple variants, on a constant basis, and crisscrossing several complex networks. The complexity of this interwoven data sources gives the cyberspace its flare as an information superhighway.

From a Cybersecurity viewpoint, the complexity and enormity of BD qualify it to own a unique version of security defenses and protections that are commensurate with its density. In an increasingly data-driven world [13], a part of the BD that is specific to humans is digital identity, often appearing as electronic digital identities (eIDs). eIDs require special classification and analysis to apportion appropriate security protections.

The next generation Cybersecurity in BD will leverage the power of AI. Machine learning algorithms designed to analyze complex data aggregates will help in predicting and neutralizing cyber scams where humans get fooled by fraudsters through impersonation. A potential application of this solution is in intercepting and decoding deep fakes and manipulated videos produced by fabricated images and sounds that appear to be real. Future Cybersecurity in BD will be able to deal with image manipulations, speech synthesis, and other artificial production of human speech intended to propagate phishing scams, social engineering hoaxes, and other cyber exploits that target human vulnerabilities.

7.1.3 Cybersecurity in Telemedicine

The potentials of future telemedicine in the post COVID-19 digital era will see a fusion of eHealth with artificial intelligence, internet of things, and big data analytics, and can only best be described as a major component of the next big thing.

The special attention received by telemedicine during the COVID-19 pandemic was a credence to its potentials to utilize high-speed data networks [14], sophisticated software algorithms, and multi-functional medical interaction platforms to provide healthcare and related services for patients without creating interfaces for direct contact by medical health workers and with each other. Teleconsultation by telephone or video was the simplest application of telemedicine during the pandemic as healthcare providers cashed in on the importance of treating patients remotely [15] to ensure safety of medical professionals.

In the US, for example, hospitals and healthcare providers activated full use of telemedicine for the remote management of coronavirus patients [16]. This followed legislative adjustments made to the US Connect for Health Act, which lifted restrictions on Medicare Telehealth coverage during emergencies in the US allowing the use of telemedicine to expand access to care and enable timely treatment, and limiting the risk of COVID-19 transmission [17, 18] from one person to the other.

As plausible as telemedicine served the pandemic's purposes, the major challenge was its disjointed nature without an adopted globally coordinated approach. With the experience of COVID-19, telemedicine's indispensable role in protecting the confidentiality, integrity, and availability of healthcare data has been further reinforced. Cybersecurity has a huge impact on post-COVID-19 telemedicine and related assets, for the following reasons:

- The envisaged size of future healthcare records.
- The complexity of future medical data.
- The expansive nature of future healthcare data.
- The unconventional sources of future health data.

Dealing with the anticipated size, complexity, nature, and sources of healthcare data requires a coordinated approach to managing electronic health record (EHR), personal health record (PHR), and aggregated health information exchange (HIE). Online support for remote healthcare delivery is an area of serious concern requiring superior data security protocols in favour of telemedicine. A combination of the following best practices [19] is recommended for practitioners, patients, and system administrators to reduce Cybersecurity risks to healthcare organizations:

- Cybersecurity awareness principles.
- Strict passwords management.
- Multi-factor authentication.
- Systems hardening.
- System security patches.
- Anti-malware software and security tools.
- Access control.
- Network segmentation.
- Continuous system monitoring and threat hunting.
- Business continuity planning.

The fragmented and unprepared approach to the application of telemedicine in a pandemic situation of the magnitude of COVID-19 left lots of loopholes that now call for refinements of its standardization.

Post COVID-19 telemedicine will see a more coordinated fusion of eHealth with the three emerging technological concepts, namely, AI, internet of things (IoT), and BD analytics, as illustrated in Figure 7.1.

Given the capabilities of AI technology [14], its optimized potentials fused with IoT and BD can be applied in future telemedicine to overcome most of the medical and social challenges created by the existing health challenges and outbreaks far beyond the magnitude of COVID-19. While it is important to exhibit caution in technological choices [20], it is even more demanding to put digital initiatives to support the management of such contemporary health challenges.

With the AI-IoT-BD fusion, collaborative video sharing that is triggered automatically by predictive data analytics is possible. This possibility could pave the way towards computer-generated anticipation of disease outbreaks based on the complex computational analysis of composite medical trends in a proactive manner. The huge data that will result from such complex analytics could potentially become the trigger that would intuitively suggest medical interventions, as well as automatically connect patients and physicians over long distances during medical emergencies and pandemics.

Diagnosis of diseases and patient treatment can be performed on time by medical experts by using advanced video conferencing [16, 21] platforms that will be tailored to medical and healthcare management principles. The potentials of future telemedicine in the post-COVID-19 digital era are inexhaustible and can only best be described as a major component of the next big thing.

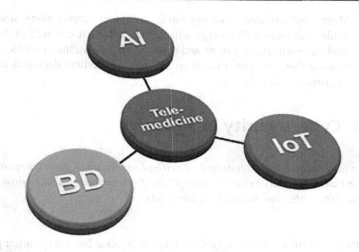

FIGURE 7.1   Future drivers of post COVID-19 telemedicine.

Post COVID-19 real-time telemedicine will see an aggregation of telecare, telehealth, teletherapy, and telemonitoring in a manner that truly brings out its diverse and huge potentials that would surpass the limitations of the social distancing protocols against the COVID-19 pandemic [16] or other future health emergencies of similar proportion. In addition to providing intelligent doctor-patient interactive solutions, it will also carry out predictive delivery of relevant medical images, and highly-automated remote patient management by a complex matching algorithm. In addition to prompt remote patient administration and cost reduction, the protection of caregivers, medical personnel and the public from contact-based infections will be one of the cardinal objectives of the post COVID-19 telemedicine.

Some predicted technological components that will fuse into future telemedicine are highlighted below:

- Chatbots will help patients find doctor availability speedily, book an appointment, and diagnose symptoms using predictive analytics of patient's pre-existing medical records held in patient-controlled repositories.
- Optimized medical wearables will automatically measure, compare, and analyze personalized medical readings, and will intuitively exchange vital healthcare data with the most suitable healthcare professionals within close vicinity, with cutting edge precision.

- More sophisticated patient-centric computer applications and medical devices will emerge with capabilities that can intuitively analyze medical conditions and detect any correlations in medications or therapy, with a focus on automating medical decisions to improve health outcomes.

7.1.4 Cybersecurity in Aviation

> *...aviation data are categorized as critical assets since their compromise can potentially result in disruption of operations, harm to property, risk to life, and jeopardy to air safety.*

Over the years, the Cybersecurity dimension of aviation has always attempted to probe what could possibly go wrong if aviation data gets compromised owing to a cyber breach, and what measures are available to predict, detect, prevent, or respond to such incidents targeted at sensitive aviation data. Aviation-related data is critical for several reasons.

Firstly, aviation data is considered very sensitive because of its association with flight safety, border crime control, airport operations security, as well as the exchange and communication of discrete navigational information. As a result, a compromise in its confidentiality, integrity, or availability can easily give pilots and air traffic controllers a false weather report or an altered traffic density that could potentially lead to a wrong decision or precipitate conditions that could result in an air disaster. Besides, there is limited interconnectivity between aviation systems, which allows for threats to potentially go undetected for months.

Secondly, an operational data breach affecting an airport's access control systems could render the biometric authentication system (BAS) incapable of detecting criminal profiles under international watch list, and this can potentially lead to high rates of false errors whereby legitimate passengers are erroneously denied access while unauthorized persons are wrongfully permitted access, respectively. While denial of legitimate individuals could be initially embarrassing, wrongfully granting access to a criminal profile owing to a cyberattack has grievous consequences, including the inadvertent onboarding of wanted terrorists into airplanes.

Thirdly, in terms of haulage and logistics, airport personnel rely on accurate and timely data to precisely determine the contents and destination of onboard luggage. Any manipulation of such data could result in misrouting of parcels among airlines. In an extreme case where a cyber breach affects an airport's automatic parcel management system, the impacts can include the under-protection of fragile luggage, including animals onboard and harmful chemical products that require special safety prerequisites for their airborne transportation.

For these reasons, all aviation data components are categorized as critical assets since their compromise can result in harm to property, risk to life, and jeopardy to air safety.

Cybersecurity as applied within the aviation sector generally provides administrative and technical guidelines for the protection of sensitive flight data and aviation records from authorized access and illegal modification, to prevent the possibility of grievous impacts on aviation systems if undetected or mitigated.

With many airports closed and international travel restrictions imposed in the aftermath of the pervasive COVID-19 lockdown and border closures, the aviation industry was one of those that were hardest hit by the COVID-19 pandemic. With closed borders and airspace suspension, domestic and international flight operations were grounded for several months as part of the measures to restrict human mobility and control the spread of the virus across geographies. Skeletal services, where necessary, were merely remotely performed by designated airport staff members who could only access company data using open networks that were less secure than the corporate networks protected by multiple layers of defense systems. The threats were enormous, the vulnerabilities were daunting, and the breaches were targeted such as the multiple website hijack at the San Francisco International Airport (SFO) in the US, as reported in March 2020 [22–24].

The complexity of Cybersecurity breaches that dominated the pandemic in diverse industries, including aviation, revealed a trend that indicates sophistication in the attack pattern resulting in a high success rate for most attacks. Many of the known attacks utilized a combination of social engineering and email phishing to perform reconnaissance and obtain initial attack data, respectively.

The aviation industry is both highly reliant on information technology and computer systems, and also vulnerable to sophisticated cyberattacks due to a combination of digital transformation, connectivity, segmentation, and complexity [25]. This trend portends a serious threat to the aviation safety and the global air travel. Besides, civil aviation is mainly reliant on cyber-enabled technologies which are used to increase safety and efficiency of air transport [26], thereby increasing the risk potentials to cyberattacks.

Cyberattacks in the aviation industry could be very complex [27], with hackers always working hard to infiltrate the computerized transport and aviation systems [28] of airlines, airports, aircraft manufacturers, and even satellites and space stations [29].

In the context of aviation, cybercrimes and cyberterrorism could affect air transport in numerous ways. For example, cyberterrorist acts could be used to spread disinformation or to engage in psychological warfare where media attention could be manipulated regarding possible threats, which would potentially cause disruption to airport and aircraft operations [30]. This could result in the "fear factor" that was an immediate aftermath of 9/11 where many persons showed great reluctance to air travel.

Post-pandemic Cybersecurity in the aviation industry will be driven by real-time data analytics relying on the gains of AI and IoT. It is time to optimize deep packet inspection as a mandatory specification for all aviation-related network devices and software applications. Intelligent deep packet inspection will perform detailed examination of network traffic involving highly sensitive electronic flight data generated and used for flight operations, including navigational systems and border control identifications. IoT support will enable interconnected aviation systems to process information faster and make better decisions [31] on safety based on the real-time data.

The Aviation Cyber Security Strategy proposed by the International Air Transport Association (IATA) is most suitable for post COVID-19 aviation Cybersecurity posture to coordinate standards, and services for cyber protection for the industry [27], bearing in mind that loss or compromise of certain classes of aviation data such as avionics [28] records could potentially result in disastrous consequences.

Furthermore, other policies and measures for the prevention and mitigation of cyber risks as jointly developed by the International Coordinating Council of Aerospace Industries Associations (ICCAIA), the Civil Air Navigation Services Organization (CANSO), and others should be applied in all airports around the world in order to shield their infrastructure, systems, and networks for the safety of aircrafts, passengers, and employees [32].

Such all-round protection is most expedient in the post COVID-19 digital era, given the stimulated awareness which the cyberspace has received in the period of the pandemic.

This projection requires global cooperation and a renewed willingness among industry players to evolve a paradigm shift in the application of Cybersecurity to prevent, detect, and proactively respond to cyber safety concerns that could potentially threaten air navigation.

7.2 CHAPTER SUMMARY

Global Cybersecurity budgets between 2021 and 2025 will shift focus towards behaviour-based Cybersecurity systems that can better anticipate data loss incidents before they occur [11]. The chain of components that constitute

AI, intelligent telemedicine, and aviation safety is multifaceted and future Cybersecurity provides assurances for trustworthy exchange of electronic data for medical administration, disease mapping, flight communications, and airport logistic operations. Cybersecurity in post COVID-19 era will leverage the potentials of AI, BD, and IoT to offer a fortified defense mechanism across industrial, academic, government, and individual computing scenarios.

REFERENCES

1. Paul Meyer, "Norms of Responsible State Behaviour in Cyberspace," in *The Ethics of Cybersecurity*, Springer, Cham, 2020, pp. 347–360. [Online]. Available: https://doi.org/10.1007/978-3-030-29053-5_18
2. UNODA, "Protecting People in Cyberspace: The Vital Role of the United Nations in 2020," Microsoft, 2020. [Online]. Available:https://www.un.org/disarmament/wp-content/uploads/2019/12/protecting-people-in-cyberspace-december-2019.pdf
3. Viostream, "UN Cyber Norms- API391202 English Subtitles," Australian Strategic Policy Institute (ASPI), 2020. [Online]. Available: https://publish.viostream.com/play/6aoztqn6edirb [Accessed 2 September 2020].
4. A.-H. Ajijola, "Interviewee," UN Norms of Responsible State Behaviour in the Cyberspace. [Interview]. 2020.
5. "Developments in the Field of Information and Telecommunications in the Context of International Security," United Nations Office for Disarmament Affiars (UNODA), December 2018. [Online]. Available: https://www.un.org/disarmament/ict-security [Accessed 2 September 2020].
6. Jacob Parker, "What is the Future of Cybersecurity?," TechRadar, 19 May 2020. [Online]. Available: https://www.techradar.com/news/what-is-the-future-of-cybersecurity [Accessed 30 August 2020].
7. Sharda. Tickoo, "Demystifying Ransomware - the Cyber Pandemic," Economic Times, 29 June 2020. [Online]. Available: https://ciso.economictimes.india-times.com/news/demystifying-ransomware-the-cyber-pandemic/76684165 [Accessed 1 July 2020].
8. Louis Columbus, "Machines Protecting Themselves Is The Future Of Cybersecurity," Forbes, 15 April 2020. [Online]. Available: https://www.forbes.com/sites/louiscolumbus/2020/04/15/machines-protecting-themselves-is-the-future-of-cybersecurity/#405759dd4457 [Accessed 30 August 2020].
9. "Future of Cybersecurity Threats – Looking Ahead So We Can Prepare Now," Security Boulevard, 17 March 2020. [Online]. Available: https://securityboulevard.com/2020/03/future-of-cybersecurity-threats-looking-ahead-so-we-can-prepare-now/ [Accessed 30 August 2020].
10. Admin, "The 7 Most Common Types of Business Technology," Zimega Technology Solutions, 27 July 2018. [Online]. Available: https://www.zimegats.com/the-7-most-common-types-of-business-technology/ [Accessed 1 August 2020].

11. Angelica Torres-Corral, "The Future of Cybersecurity is Proactive, Predictive and Dynamic," Forcepoint, 13 January 2020. [Online]. Available: https://www.forcepoint.com/blog/insights/the-future-of-cybersecurity-proactive-predictive-dynamic [Accessed 30 August 2020].

12. Heather Zeiger, "China: What You Didn't Say Could Be Used Against You," Mind Matters, 26 August 2019. [Online]. Available: https://mindmatters.ai/2019/08/china-what-you-didnt-say-could-be-used-against-you/ [Accessed 23 May 2020].

13. D. Reinsel, J. Gantz and J. Rydning, "The digitization of the world: From edge to core," IDC, Framingham, Massachusetts, 2018.

14. Z. Mastaneh and Ali Mouseli, "Technology and its solutions in the era of COVID-19 crisis: A review of literature.," *Evidence Based Health Policy, Management & Economics*, vol. 4, no. 2, pp. 138–149, 2020.

15. World Government Summit, "How Technology is Changing the Health Sector," YouTube, 12 April 2017. [Online]. Available: https://youtu.be/cM4aep7VXb8 [Accessed 18 June 2020].

16. K. U. Okereafor, O. Adebola and R. Djehaiche, "Exploring the potentials of telemedicine and other non-contact electronic health technologies in controlling the spread of the novel Coronavirus Disease (COVID-19)," *International Journal in IT & Engineering*, vol. 8, no. 4, pp. 1–11, 2020.

17. Mike Miliard, "Congress waives Telehealth Restrictions for Coronavirus Screening," Healthcare IT News, 2020. [Online]. Available: https://www.healthcareitnews.com/news/congress-waives-telehealth-restrictions-coronavirus-screening [Accessed 28 March 2020].

18. A. Klein, L. Kulp and A. Sarcevic, "Designing and optimizing digital applications for medical emergencies," Drexel University, Philadelphia, 2018.

19. NJCCIC Advisory, "Cyber Threats & Cybersecurity for Healthcare During COVID-19," New Jersey Cybersecurity and Communications Integration Cell (NJCCIC), 8 April 2020. [Online]. Available: https://www.cyber.nj.gov/alerts-advisories/cyber-threats-cybersecurity-for-healthcare-during-covid-19 [Accessed 5 August 2020].

20. K. U. Okereafor and O. Adebola, "Tackling the cybersecurity impacts of the coronavirus outbreak as a challenge to internet safety," *International Journal in IT and Engineering (IJITE)*, vol. 8, no. 2, pp. 1–14, 2020.

21. T. Tebeje and J. Klein, "Applications of e-health to support person-centered health care at the time of COVID-19 pandemic," Telemedicine and eHealth, 31 July, 2020. [Online]. Available: https://doi.org/10.1089/tmj.2020.0201 [Accessed 1 August, 2020]

22. Duncan Riley, "Login Credentials Stolen in Hack of San Francisco International Airport Websites," Silicon Angle, 12 April 2020. [Online]. Available: https://siliconangle.com/2020/04/12/login-credentials-stolen-hack-san-francisco-international-airport-websites/ [Accessed 1 August 2020].

23. Davey Winder, "San Francisco Airport Cyber Attack Confirmed: Windows Passwords Stolen," Forbes, 11 April 2020. [Online]. Available: https://www.forbes.com/sites/daveywinder/2020/04/11/san-francisco-airport-cyber-attack-confirmed-windows-passwords-stolen/#608b75125b9c [Accessed 31 July 2020].

24. "San Francisco Airport Data Breach: Double Website Hack may have Lifted Users' Windows login credentials," The Daily Swig, 14 April 2020. [Online]. Available: https://portswigger.net/daily-swig/san-francisco-airport-data-breach-double-website-hack-may-have-lifted-users-windows-login-credentials [Accessed 1 August 2020].

25. "Cyber Threats to the Aviation Industry: Why Cyber Criminals are Targeting the Aviation Industry," Cyber Risk International, 2020. [Online]. Available: https://cyberriskinternational.com/2020/04/06/cyber-threats-to-the-aviation-industry/ [Accessed 12 August 2020].

26. "Civil Aviation Cybersecurity," International Civil Aviation Organization (ICAO), 2020. [Online]. Available: https://www.icao.int/cybersecurity/Pages/default.aspx [Accessed 12 August 2020].

27. "Aviation Cyber Security," International Air Transport Association (IATA), Montreal, Canada, 2020.

28. Roberto Sabatini, "Cyber Security in the Aviation Context," in First Cyber Security Workshop, Melbourne, Australia, 2016.

29. "Cyberattacks in the Aviation Industry," AVLAW Consulting, 2020. [Online]. Available: https://avlaw.com.au/cyberattacks-aviation-industry/ [Accessed 12 August 2020].

30. Ruwantissa Abeyratne, "Cyber Terrorism and Aviation—National and International Responses," Journal of Transportation Security, vol. 4, no. 4, pp. 337–349, 2011.

31. Eve De Clerk, "How do Airports Remain Safe against the Constant Threat of Cyber-attacks?" International Airport Review, 29 August 2019. [Online]. Available: https://www.internationalairportreview.com/article/100777/airports-remain-safe-constant-threat-cyber-attacks/ [Accessed 23 August 2020].

32. Maria Kossena, "Cyber Security in Air Transportation," University of the Aegean, Greece, Mytilene, 2019.

Conclusion and Recommendations

8

The good side of COVID-19 is the rise in global Cybersecurity consciousness, as organizations have now evolved new ways of working that are more technology-dependent than ever.

As the world waited frantically for COVID-19 remedies including vaccines [1], and as every online information referencing "coronavirus" became attractive, cyber criminals exploited the fear and uncertainty, distributed malicious software, and carried out phishing campaign that compromised data and disrupted digital operations across sectors. Some big lessons are worth highlighting.

8.1 REMOTE WORK COMES TO STAY

The pandemic ushered in a new worldwide culture, one that has changed the way people work and collaborate, threatened the way people live and communicate [2], but interestingly fostered greater cyber resilience and unprecedented digital dependency [3]. The pandemic sparked new paradigms of human interactions at all levels. The threat of the COVID-19 virus forced companies worldwide into a hurried shift to remote working [4], a move which left workers and employees at risks of increased cyberattacks.

As COVID-19 emphasized on online security and remote work, it is now time to sanitize the etiquettes of the work from home (WFH) paradigm, now popularized by the reality of the pandemic that forced many organizations to reevaluate their operational models and consider electronic alternatives to corporate business processes. Fixing loopholes in WFH creates business opportunities for technology vendors, and provides more assurance to online consumers. The outcome will produce safer cyberspace for leisure, commerce, family, education, and healthcare.

As changes to work practices and socialization meant spending increased periods of time online [2], the WFH concept brought about a shift in focus for hackers [5] to end users, most of whose systems do not possess adequate protection to cope with the new cyberattack [6] dynamics and business alterations. With altered business processes and new economic realities, post COVID-19 pandemic working life will never remain the same again.

Forcing billions of people to stay at, and work from, home was ideal for curbing the pandemic, but it also promoted cybercrime against weak defenses. This calls for strengthening of national and international cyber defense policies [7]. The big lesson lies in understanding how to carry out remote work more securely using a mix of Cybersecurity ethics, workforce psychology, and predictive analytics powered by big data technology.

8.2 CRYPTOGRAPHIC AND STEGANOGRAPHIC REMEDIES

Protecting sensitive data is more profitable than responding a cyberattack amid huge consequences. Apart from the qualitative and revenue cost of incident response, the loss of business competitive advantage for organizations and leakage of personal information for individuals could become unbearable in the aftermath of a cyberattack.

COVID-19 was a wake-up call to redefine data protection that strives to maximize the potentials of cryptography and steganography as methods of protecting critical data in storage, or in transit. While cryptography protects data in transit by presenting its content in a manner meaningless to an attacker, steganography hides sensitive data within another data by concealing its appearance from plain sight recognition.

Cryptography requires keys for its processes – encryption key for scrambling data, and decryption key for reassembling an encrypted data. These keys are computer security codes and algorithms that are generated and shared using a secure framework – the public key infrastructure (PKI). PKI of the post COVID-19 era needs optimization for greater impact.

Post pandemic PKI optimization should explore a systematic combination of cryptography and steganography as a consolidated technique for providing robust protection for sensitive data moving across multiple networks.

8.3 NEW CONCEPT OF MONITORING AND SURVEILLANCE

COVID-19 Cybersecurity trends revealed that more data networks require surveillance for proactive detection of potential indicators of compromise. Both individual devices and organization networks require a structured monitoring and alert strategy to forestall the huge consequences that follow successful breaches.

Existing monitoring technologies need to be used ethically for maximum efficiency. As a result, a shift in the concept of ethical monitoring and surveillance over data networks is inevitable for detecting indicators of cybercrime and other hostile activities in advance [6] and for preventing undesirable consequences.

8.4 MORE STRINGENT EMAIL POLICIES

The two major reasons for the preference of email over surface mailing – security and convenience – now appear to be facing a big blow. The email system is becoming increasingly vulnerable to phishing, spamming, and confidence tricks as typified during the pandemic, resulting in the high rate of business email compromises (BEC) recorded. This raises trust issues over the ability of the current email security architecture to withstand the pressure of constantly being exploited by spammers as malware distribution agent.

The current state of the email system does not indicate the capability to cope with the projected sophistication of future cyberattacks and the situation is not likely to decline, especially given the evolution of emerging big data and internet of things (IoT) concepts.

The email system is chronically susceptible to social engineering campaigns that characterized many of the COVID-19 incidents, in addition to its proneness to misconfigurations [8] and internal vulnerabilities. Such hiccups require a review of its current design and implementation modalities.

8.4.1 Proposed Design Model for Email Security Re-engineering

A novel combination of technical and administrative countermeasures is required to redefine existing email protocols and redesign email systems to respond more intuitively to suspicious patterns indicative of attack profile.

An AI-based predictive analytics engine is recommended to be embedded in the simple mail transfer protocol (SMTP) to proactively scan for suspicious patterns (updated from the email vulnerability database) as a routine operational procedure. The redesigned architecture should offer a variety of automated suggestions to the user on optional action(s) to support decision to open or ignore a flagged email message. This should be integrated alongside the email filtering capabilities to optimize security and reduce false negatives.

8.4.2 Implementation Strategy for Email Security Re-engineering

The optimized implementation of the email security frameworks should be made extensible and dynamic to accommodate intuitive features for automated actions during occasions of sudden flood of hostile messages such as seen in the BEC of COVID-19. The long-term implementation strategy would require a three-prong approach comprising of the following:

- Collation of inputs and aggregation of user comments on email re-engineering.
- Industry commitment to shift to a more secure and robust email system.
- Multi-sectoral risk analysis to simulate potential impacts of implementing an optimized system.

8.5 PUNISHMENT FOR MALWARE-RELATED OFFENCES

There does not seem to be enough criminal deterrent measures against ransomware and other destructive malware attacks, and this loophole emboldens perpetrators. As a result, the risk vs. reward balance always tilts in favour of the criminals. According to the CrowdStrike's 2020 Global Threat Report [9], this merciless ransomware epidemic will continue and is likely to worsen, as long as the practice remains lucrative, and relatively easy and risk-free.

While country and regional laws define cybercrimes to suite their geo-cultural sensitivities and to complement enforcement boundaries, global legislations and treaties seem to be clueless and vague on dealing with ransomware offenders. This might be because of its abstract mode of perpetration or the difficulty in establishing culpability via evidence-based detection of attacker's identity.

There is a huge stigma associated with paying ransoms [10], in addition to tax deduction crises. Besides, it also fuels the cybercrime industry and could encourage future attacks. Since the taking of money [11], in this case ransom money, or property through fraud, misrepresentation, or coercion is regarded as theft so long as it is illegal under state or local laws, suggested remedies for punishing ransomware offender should include the following:

- Optimized technological capabilities for tracking ransom payments and apprehending suspected criminals that are linked to initiation and receipt of such payments.
- Adoption of more stringent penalties for convicted offenders.
- Classification of intentional cyberattacks on critical infrastructure as acts of terrorism.
- Other variants could treat physical harm or death arising from cyberattacks as assault, attempted murder, and invoke murder-related charges as appropriate.

Ultimately, the most impactful method to stop ransomware is to refrain from paying the ransoms [12], thereby making the business unprofitable and unattractive. In addition, it is the responsibility of the organization to safeguard critical elements of its digital life, so carting out a routine backup of the most valuable information should be made a mandatory aspect of the post-COVID-19 digital ethics.

8.6 ACCULTURATION OF SOCIAL ENGINEERING

A major Cybersecurity fallout of COVID-19 crisis was the association of the rise in cybercrimes rates to social engineering, especially using email as a tool. Social engineering is the art of tricking humans by taking advantage of their weaknesses including ignorance, fear, panic, and loyalty to obtain sensitive data that could be used to carry out malicious activities such as identity theft and cyber espionage. Due to ignorance of the gimmicks of social engineering, aggravated by the uncertainty and panic over the pandemic, cyber criminals exploited human weaknesses in many forms to obtain confidential information from unsuspecting victims.

Victims succumbed to social engineering pranks due to a combination of limited knowledge and panic, both of which could be addressed if the requisite capacity to detect and prevent social engineering is fused into our daily activities. One of the strongest defenses is to invest in training to aid personnel in identifying risks and thwarting security incidents.

It is time to make social engineering consciousness a global way of life, a style of living, and a mandatory cyber ethics adjustment through acculturation. Acculturation of social engineering should focus on cultural modification processes in which employees and cyberspace consumers would adopt, adapt, acquire, and adjust to new orientations in cyber ethics within similar or different environments. Instead of merely building strong technical defenses around the facilities where data is stored, forward-looking organizations could go a step further to protect and sensitize the employees who generate, access, and share critical data [13]. Since consumers and employees are the critical link in the Cybersecurity chain, an organization's information security strategy must be mandatorily focused to identify and mitigate the human factor risks by developing safeguards to protect both data and networks.

8.6.1 Proposed Implementation Model for Social Engineering Acculturation

Achieving social engineering acculturation requires a coordinated global approach in which prime institutions could take up chunks of this technological challenge and foster their propagation using the influence of their institutional mandates across continental, regional, industrial, and professional affiliations. This is achievable by creating ecosystems of universal, non-domineering, time-limited initiatives that can interact seamlessly across schemes, sectors, countries, and borders.

While some institutions are focusing on global advocacy for acculturation of social engineering, others may be pushing for legislative paradigms across global jurisdictions, and yet others could go for diplomatic channels. For example, the United Nations International Telecommunication Union (ITU) can invoke and reinvigorate the fourth pillar (capacity building) and the fifth pillar (international cooperation) of its Global Cybersecurity Agenda (GCA) to raise global Cybersecurity awareness and promote countries' participation in Cybersecurity collaborations, respectively, across industries and sectors.

If these strategic measures are well-coordinated on a global scale including the UN's promotion of the norms of responsible state behaviour in the cyberspace [14, 15], the positive outcomes could become evident in the short term, and would result in long-term decline in social engineering. The UN norms of responsible state behaviour in the cyberspace prove helpful in developing national Cybersecurity policies and strategies that are contextually relevant and rooted in international good practice [16–18], including social engineering acculturation. The norms also describe what countries should and should not be doing in the cyberspace. The fourth pillar of the UN norms of responsible state behaviour in the cyberspace is cyber capacity building to ensure that all 193 UN member states can harness the benefits and mitigate the risks of increased connectivity [18].

Beyond achieving Cybersecurity harmony, social engineering acculturation also has the additional advantage of impacting both social and psychological well-being on the cyberspace, in addition to striking a balance between risk aversion and risk appetite on the parts of both vendors and consumers of Cybersecurity products and services.

8.7 BETTER MANAGEMENT OF DIGITAL IDENTITY (DID)

Although digital identities are usually held in trust by data management institutions for the provision of data-on-demand services for verification seekers under strict privacy regulations, there is a huge knowledge gap in the handling of digital identities even among data management institutions. This raises serious security concerns over compliance with those Cybersecurity ethics that pertain to the exchange of personally identifiable information (PII).

The current identity system is still flawed with overbearing state surveillance alongside disclosure of unwanted metadata to verification seekers, a practice that has so become commonplace that it is almost generally accepted as the norm, albeit regrettably. If the practice remains unchecked, both eID owners and verifications seekers can become endangered by surveillance by state security forces, law enforcement, terrorists, organized crime gangs, and non-state actors.

There are also doubts over the relevance of introducing commercial intermediaries between citizens and access to their public services with data management institutions under whose custody their Digital Identities (DiDs) are entrusted in confidence. It is hereby recommended that counter- and anti-surveillance capabilities be integrated into the digital identity ecosystems to enable eID owners to both detect surveillance and take the most appropriate actions.

Limiting the minimum volume of information that must be released as a person's digital identity attributes rather than revealing everything about own past and history could reduce the amount of personal data taken and potentially lost or misused by organizations during interactions, including hostile cyberattacks.

Better strategy and tactics are required to solve these problems, and address the following questions:

- Do we necessarily need to prove our identity always?
- How best can digital identities authenticate us with minimal information without revealing more than enough private information about us, e.g., using zero knowledge proof?
- How best can a compromised digital identity be mitigated and safely reused without fear of identity theft, impersonation, and incessant spoofing?

Tackling these questions will lead the way into fashioning a better management of digital identities.

There is need for a more convenient and effective solution to the management of DiDs, one that allows citizens to manage their own identity-related data and choose where, when, and with whom they share it [19] without overbearing restrictions. Limiting the choice of DiD exchange to identity managers alone creates a loophole that can potentially promote high-profile cyber espionage, surveillance, and credential racketeering. Without user control over own data, incidents of privacy breaches and identity theft may remain on the increase, leaving the cyberspace more porous and unreliable.

Since trusted online relationships are essential to the digital economy, every user reserves the right to see and possibly edit any information about themselves [20] regarding the provision of accurate and up-to-date data, and in line with one of the ten principles of self-sovereignty, *"persistence"*. This is the purpose for which an audit trail is kept for preserving records of present and past identity data.

It is time to ramp up the decentralized ID foundation by invoking multiple elements of security concepts. There should be a more balanced way to take advantage of different security mechanisms to protect users' accounts against fraud and hacks, rather than forcing them to prove their identity by answering questions to authenticate their claimed identity. This initiative can benchmark a semblance of Capital One's Swift ID solution which authenticates users with just a swipe on the smartphone's screen [21, 22].

From a DiD security viewpoint, a properly secured approach to managing the interdependencies between digital identities and the huge data generated from emerging technology concepts could potentially guarantee non-surveillance, and non-intrusive record of who, where, when, and with whom we have disclosed our data. The resulting citizen-controlled and self-managed digital identity would make online transactions safer, and reduce malware attacks that have hitherto remained skewed towards social engineering, repudiation, forgery, and malicious misuse of personal data.

8.7.1 Requirements for Better Digital Identity Management

The emerging digital era will rely on secure identification, and Cybersecurity will play a leading role in identity protection and management given the rapid evolution of many national identity schemes. The identity used by citizens to interact with government, access services, or pay for goods is highly vulnerable, and so requires better management.

While many national identity schemes exist as either foundational or functional, they all have one thing in common – they all require initial data onboarding either by direct capture from citizens or by acquisition from the harmonization of silos of electronic identities existing in multiple repositories. Digital interactions are based on trust [23], and digital identities as fundamental to that trust.

All actors within the digital identity ecosystem, including vendors of identity applications, should promote rather than discourage the inclusion of privacy-enhancing security features in their products, services, and advisories to reflect the following:

- Interoperability
- Minimal disclosure
- Anti-surveillance
- Counter-surveillance
- Identity reciprocity
- Owner-dependent control
- Need to know
- Zero knowledge proof

These security features will consolidate on privacy and minimize the impact of data breaches anytime they occur. As a result, there should be no monitoring by government or other organizations of where, when, and with whom digital identity is used [19]. Identity should be about precisely proof of something about self, not surveillance by government, companies, or other organizations.

As countries and regions adopt unique identity management protocols that are both suitable to them and interoperable with global standards, all Cybersecurity initiatives on digital identities revolve around the manner in which their confidentiality, integrity, and availability are protected and securely managed across the entire data life cycle. They also relate to the standardization of the digital identity supply chain. Digital identity should therefore focus on precisely providing identity proof through the use of open standards and transparent verification [24], while devoid of state or private sector tracking, surveillance, and control.

In summary, there is need to evolve, in the post-pandemic era, a new generation of digital credentials that offers transformative convenience and security for all stakeholders offering a new public infrastructure for verifying credentials in a manner far more durable, secure, and convenient than relying upon a single authority.

8.8 LAST LINE

Post-pandemic digital era looks very promising, even as COVID-19 left a huge Cybersecurity impact on the digital behaviour [25] of digital consumers and internet users not only in the directly affected localities but across the globe. While counting the losses, a significant proportion of the lessons should be focused on preparedness on the side of global cyber response to such a major event. Secure management and user control of digital identities, for example, should become an indispensable global priority.

With the fresh lessons from the pandemic, and the proposals offered in this book, the equitable use of digital technology would be transformed for good, rather than wait for the next pandemic. A sanitized Cybersecurity outlook awaits in the horizon with plenty of benefits for internet users, online commerce operators, security vendors, governments, cyberspace consumers, Cybersecurity scholars, and consequential beneficiaries.

We must all play our roles as individuals, organizations, nations, and societies to be conscious of the risks we take on the internet, and to recognize and react promptly to the threats that we face on the cyberspace. Doing this will guarantee that Cybersecurity propagates a safer cyberspace for leisure, family, work, and business in the post COVID-19 digital era, an era that will witness a new version of Cybersecurity fully optimized to intuitively neutralize the sophistication of contemporary cyberattacks.

REFERENCES

1. R. Zhang, Y. Li, A. L. Zhang, Y. Wang and M. J. Molina, "Identifying airborne transmission as the dominant route for the spread of COVID-19," *Proceedings of the National Academy of Sciences (PNAS) of the United States of America*, vol. 117, no. 26, pp. 14857–14863, 2020.
2. H. S. Lallie, L. A. Shepherd, J. R. C. Nurse, A. Erola, G. Epiphaniou, C. Maple and X. Bellekens, "Cyber security in the age of COVID-19: A timeline and analysis of cyber-crime and cyber-attacks during the pandemic," arXiv:2006.11929v1 [cs.CR], pp. 1–19, 2020.
3. A. Russo, "Dramatic Rise of Cybersecurity Risks from COVID-19 Prompts Action Plan," World Economic Forum, 26 May 2020. [Online]. Available: https://www.weforum.org/press/2020/05/dramatic-rise-of-cybersecurity-risks-from-covid-19-prompts-action-plan/ [Accessed 31 July 2020].
4. Global Data Thematic Research, "Cybersecurity: Timeline," The Verdict, 6 July 2020. [Online]. Available: https://www.verdict.co.uk/cybersecurity-timeline/ [Accessed 30 July 2020].
5. C. Onwuegbuchi, "Expert Blames Fundamental Flaw in IP for Cyberattacks," Nigeria Communications Week, 13 July 2020. [Online]. Available: https://www.nigeriacommunicationsweek.com.ng/expert-blames-fundamental-flaw-in-ip-for-cyberattacks/ [Accessed 13 July 2020].
6. K. Okereafor and O. Adelaiye, "Randomized cyber attack simulation model: A cybersecurity mitigation proposal for Post COVID-19 digital era," *International Journal of Recent Engineering Research and Development (IJRERD)*, vol. 05, no. 07, pp. 61–72, 2020.
7. D. E. Denning, "Activism, hacktivism, and cyberterrorism: the internet as a tool for influencing foreign policy," in *Networks and Netwars: The Future of Terror, Crime, and Militancy*, RAND, Santa Monica, CA, 2001, pp. 239–288.
8. "Sophos 2020 Threat Report," Sophos, Abingdon, UK, 2020.
9. G. Kurtz, "*Crowdstrike global threat report 2020*," CrowdStrike, Sunnyvale, California, 2020.
10. L. Irwin, "Avon's UK website offline a week after suffering cyberattack," IT Governance, 17 June 2020. [Online]. Available: https://www.itgovernance.co.uk/blog/avons-uk-website-offline-a-week-after-suffering-cyber-attack [Accessed 3 August 2020].
11. R. W. Wood, "Garmin Hack's $10M Ransom Payment, $10M Tax Deduction," Forbes, 27 July 2020. [Online]. Available: https://www.forbes.com/sites/robertwood/2020/07/27/garmin-hacks-10m-ransom-payment-10m-tax-deduction/#2647948412c5 [Accessed 3 August 2020].

12. D. Balaban, "Attacked by Ransomware? Here's Why You Shouldn't Pay Up," Hackernoon, 22 July 2019. [Online]. Available: https://hackernoon. com/attacked-by-ransomware-heres-why-you-shouldnt-pay-up-ma9k3x3y [Accessed 3 August 2020].

13. A. Torres-Corral, "The Future of Cybersecurity is Proactive, Predictive and Dynamic," Forcepoint, 13 January 2020. [Online]. Available: https://www. forcepoint.com/blog/insights/the-future-of-cybersecurity-proactive-predictive-dynamic [Accessed 30 August 2020].

14. P. Meyer, "Norms of responsible state behaviour in cyberspace," in *The Ethics of Cybersecurity*, Springer, Cham, vol 21, 2020, pp. 347–360. [Online]. Available: https://doi.org/10.1007/978-3-030-29053-5_18

15. UNODA, "Protecting People in Cyberspace: The Vital Role of the United Nations in 2020," Microsoft. [Online]. Available:https://www.un.org/disarmament/ wp-content/uploads/2019/12/protecting-people-in-cyberspace-december-2019. pdf, 2020

16. Viostream, "UN Cyber Norms-API391202 English Subtitles," Australian Strategic Policy Institute (ASPI), 2020. [Online]. Available: https://publish. viostream.com/play/6aoztqn6edirb [Accessed 2 September 2020].

17. A.-H. Ajijola, Interviewee, *UN Norms of Responsible State Behaviour in the Cyberspace*. [Interview]. 2020.

18. "Developments in the Field of Information and Telecommunications in the Context of International Security," United Nations Office for Disarmament Affiars (UNODA), December 2018. [Online]. Available: https://www.un.org/ disarmament/ict-security [Accessed 2 September 2020].

19. J. Fishenden, "Implementing a 21st Century Approach to Digital Identity," 8 January 2020. [Online]. Available: https://www.computerweekly.com/opinion/ Implementing-a-21st-century-approach-to-digital-identity [Accessed 16 May 2020].

20. DFI, "Digital Frontiers Institute Courses," Digital Frontiers Institute, 2020. [Online]. Available: https://www.digitalfrontiersinstitute.org/courses/ [Accessed 12 August 2020].

21. S. Perez, "Capital One Launches SwiftID, a Way to Bypass Security Questions with Just a Swipe," Tech Crunch, 23 October 2015. [Online]. Available: https:// techcrunch.com/2015/10/23/capital-one-launches-swiftid-a-way-to-bypass-security-questions-with-just-a-swipe/ [Accessed 26 May 2020].

22. Capital One, "International wire transfer guide," *Capital One, McLean*, 2016.

23. *"Digital Identity: Restoring Trust in a Digital World,"* MasterCard, New York, 2019.

24. Hyland, "Hyland Credentials," Hyland, 2020. [Online]. Available: https://www. hylandcredentials.com/ [Accessed 26 May 2020].

25. K. U. Okereafor and O. Adebola, "Tackling the cybersecurity impacts of the coronavirus outbreak as a challenge to internet safety," *International Journal in IT and Engineering (IJITE)*, vol. 8, no. 2, pp. 1–14, 2020.

Caveat

The conclusions and views expressed in this book are the author's personal opinions and do not necessarily represent the opinions of any organization(s) to which he is affiliated.

Name(s) of specific vendor(s), manufacturer(s), product(s), or institution(s) wherever mentioned or implied are for illustrative, educational, and informational purposes only. Implicit or expressed mention of such names does not suggest their endorsement or recommendation by the author.

Any comments should be emailed to the author at nitelken@yahoo.com

Glossary

9/11: 9/11 represents the September 11, 2001 attacks against the United States during which Islamic terrorists, believed to be part of the Al-Qaeda network, hijacked four commercial airplanes and crashed two of them into the World Trade Center in New York City and a third one into the Pentagon in Virginia: the fourth plane crashed into a field in rural Pennsylvania. 9/11 claimed 2,996 lives including the 19 hijackers. In the wake of the incident, several reforms emanated including the promulgation of the US PATRIOT ACT of October 26, 2001, which led to the adoption of various biometric Cybersecurity technologies for global aviation control, immigrants' management, and automated surveillance.

Adware: Malware threat that disguises as a marketing ad for an unsolicited service or product often through online pop-ups.

Anonymity: The act of hiding or concealing an identity or user profile. It is a serious Cybersecurity issue as cyber criminals tend to hide their online identity to avoid recognition.

Big data: The concept of representing very large volumes of data from multiple sources in a format that facilitates convenient data extraction, management, and analysis.

Biometric Authentication System: An electronic information system used primarily to provide biometric authentication using physiological or behavioural characteristics to verify the identity of human entities for the purpose of access control or identity matching.

Bitcoin: A cryptographically-secured digital currency, that is almost impossible to fake, double-spend, or repudiate. Bitcoin was invented in 2008 by an unknown person or group of people using the name Satoshi Nakamoto. Bitcoin promotes anonymity, hence most ransomware cyberattackers prefer to use it to receive their ransom to evade detection.

Blog: Short for web log. An online forum where members post and discuss specific topics and exchange relevant ideas.

Brute force: The use of a password-guessing tool (or a cracker) that uses a complex algorithm to try different combinations of characters with the hope of guessing correctly. The tool systematically checks all possible passwords and passphrases until the correct one is found after a period determined by the length of the password, the complexity of the character combinations, and the processing power of the cracker.

Credential: A combined set of particulars which a user presents to an information system as a login prerequisite to obtaining access. For example, Id number + password, username + PIN number. Biometric attributes can also form part of credentials in a multi-factor authentication scheme.

Cryptography: The practice of protecting an electronic message, data, or information by securely transforming its contents into a format that is unintelligible and meaningless to third parties or adversaries that intercept it in transit or in storage. A file or data is said to be encrypted if it is protected using a cryptographic technique. Cryptographic techniques ensure secure communications across networks allowing only the sender and intended recipient of an electronic message to view the contents using a shared secret key that converts the encrypted file or data into plain text, in a process called decryption, and vice-versa.

Cyber bullying: The use of digital assets to victimize, harass or disseminate falsehood and offensive content against an individual, group, or corporate organization, by hiding under the anonymity of online platforms, blogs, and forums.

Cyber espionage: The use of online techniques to spy on the digital behaviour or online transactions of an individual or a corporate organization through social engineering, spyware, shoulder surfing, cyber stalking, man-in-the-middle, brute-force, keylogging, eavesdropping or other methods.

Dark web: The hidden internet usually characterized by illegal activities including cybercrime, trades in drugs, stolen financial data, firearms, and other clandestine activities. Dark web requires specific software, configurations, or authorization to access. It is also called darknet or deep web.

Deep fake: Manipulated video using artificial intelligence to synthesize fake motions that mimic the original actions or expressions of the person being impersonated. Deep fakes are a major Cybersecurity threat as they can be potentially exploited in social engineering to inflict cyber bullying on victims and groups.

Dictionary attack: A cyberattack in which the hacker uses a password-guessing tool (or password cracker) to recover a password by trying different combinations of all words in the dictionary of different languages.

Encryption: The use of a secret key or algorithm to represent a software, code, or data in a way that cannot be reconstructed or understood by third parties or those who do not possess the key. When an electronic message, software, code, or data undergoes encryption as a protection, it is referred to as encrypted. If it is encrypted due to ransomware attack, it is said to have been locked.

Hacker: Any person or group with the skills and abilities to bypass available security controls and defense measures, and break into computers and digital assets. A person that can perfume hacking for good intentions with owner's permission is called an ethical hacker. Performing hacking for harmful or exploitative intents without the owner's permission is a form of cyberattack, and a person that engages in unauthorized hacking is called a malicious hacker.

Hacktivist: A hacktivist (hacker activist) uses hacking as a tool to obstruct normal computer activity as a form of civil disobedience to promote a political agenda or social change. Hacktivist groups use the same tools and techniques as malicious hackers to attack computer systems and disrupt services only for political reasons without emphasis on profit, fun or data theft. Hacktivists do not target causing injury or significant monetary loss but focus on using cyberattack techniques such as hacking to attract attention to a political or social cause. Hacktivism heavily relies on the internet being relatively difficult to censor and mostly anonymous.

ICT policy: A corporate ICT management document in which an organization outlines its administrative rules for technology governance, and provides a guide on the selection, acquisition, deployment, safe use and maintenance of its ICT assets, infrastructure and services over the specific lifetime of the document.

Logic bomb: Harmful malware that remains completely passive on an infected system, and only gets triggered by a pre-scheduled activity, such as upon sighting the search word "COVID-19", or upon a file attaining a certain age.

Malicious hacker: One that hacks for negative or harmful reasons including to steal data for sale, cause disruption, demand ransom or push a political ideology. A malicious hacker typically breaks into victim's computers and digital assets without permission.

Malware: Short for **mal**icious soft**ware**. A hostile and destructive computer software code designed by the cyber criminal to cause undesirable outcome, disrupt normal operations, harm functionalities or damage data structure on the victim's computer or digital asset including unauthorized access and illegal data alteration. For example, a computer virus, ransomware, Trojan horse, etc.

Man-in-the-middle attack: A session hijacking cyberattack where the intruder inserts in-between two or more parties who believe that their communication is closed loop but are unaware that their conversations and data exchanges are being intercepted and/or altered by the adversary for malicious intent.

Open data: A set of data which an organization or group of collaborators are willing, or agree, to share on a common platform for collaborative use by stakeholders with the understanding that such set of data does not infringe on the privacy right of the owners neither does it constitute any Cybersecurity concerns. Open data does not include some PIIs used in healthcare, crime investigation, legal prosecution, immigration, and aviation.

Password chaos: The confusion of having to remember a complex password or many passwords, each for a different application.

Password fatigue: The unsafe action users take to avoid password chaos e.g. reusing an old password, choosing weak combinations, writing a password on paper for safety, sharing a password with children, colleagues, friends, and associates; or worst of all by simply choosing the "*no password*" option.

Personally Identifiable Information (PII): Any piece of information or set of data that identifies or defines a person, distinguishes one person from another, or able to trace an individual's identity, and is considered private or confidential to him. E.g. financial information, biometric data, phone number, etc. Due to their sensitive nature, PIIs require adequate Cybersecurity protections to preserve their confidentiality, integrity, and availability, as well as manage their collation, storage, exchange, use and disposal.

PHI: Protected Health Information. See Protected Health Information.

Piggybacking: The act of using the privileges and benefits of an already authenticated user. Piggybacking becomes a tool in the hands of the social engineer who is desperate to trick an unsuspecting user to divulge his login credentials using threat, deceptive appeal, disguised as consent.

PII: Personally Identifiable Information. See Personally Identifiable Information.

Protected Health Information: Any personal health status information produced, used, or revealed while providing healthcare service, to identify an individual in a medical record. It includes all private medical information about an individual concerning diagnosis, prescription, treatment, health insurance, or payment for healthcare. For example, medical laboratory results, medical appointment dates, health plan beneficiary's identity numbers, names of biological relatives, etc.

Pseudonymity: The act of assuming a different or misleading identity, an alias or nickname on an online or digital platform either for deception or experimentation.

Ransomware: Malware designed to deny access to an infected computer system or data or threatens to publish the victim's data until a ransom is paid often within a specified short period of time.

Reconnaissance: The practice of obtaining background information about the security posture of a system, particularly its vulnerabilities, for the purpose of gaining enough options prior to attack. Cyberattackers use reconnaissance to spy on a target and to acquire pre-attack information they consider vital for a successful exploit. Conversely, Cybersecurity professionals and cyberattack defenders use reconnaissance to perform a comprehensive and painstaking scan of a system or entire architecture to identify weak points that could pose danger, and then proffer ethical solutions to them.

Shoulder surfing: The malicious practice of spying or looking over someone's shoulder to capture login credentials or personal/sensitive information from the keystrokes or pattern entered on an electronic device, keyboard, or application login portal.

Single sign-on: A user authentication technique whereby a single login session automatically grants the user access to all other applications to which he is authorized to access without requiring separate login credentials for each respective application. SSO is one of the remedies to password fatigue.

Spear phishing: An unsolicited and deceptive email that impersonates known brands and high-profile personalities, with the intention to extract confidential information or propagate other malware[1].

Steganography: The study of techniques for disguising an electronic message, data, information, or file (including image, audio, and video) within another file of similar or different type. Steganographic techniques are used to hide the presence of a message from third parties and eavesdropping adversaries.

Tailgating: The malicious use of others' login privileges obtained without their consent often using brute force or any hostile means or application. Together with piggybacking, shoulder surfing and eavesdropping, tailgating is a notorious technique which cyber criminals use for advancing their social engineering exploits.

Threat hunting: A phased cyber defense process used to proactively search for, detect, and neutralize patterns that indicate cyberattack potentials. Threat hunting helps to detect cyber threats that can evade existing Cybersecurity controls in a data network.

Trojan horse: A hostile malware code often disguised as a legitimate or useful downloadable software, which misleads unsuspecting users of its true intent and deploys a destructive code in an infected system.

Two-Factor Authentication: Also denoted as 2FA, a two-factor authentication is the use of two elements of user verification for added security. For example, the combination of password and biometrics, or the combination of unique token and password, etc. Using more than two such elements of verification for even higher security is known as multi-factor authentication.

Vector: Any agent that helps a virus or other malware to infect a vulnerable system. For example, an infected removable drive such as a flash drive, HDD, etc.

Virus: Malware that modifies other computer programs and inserts its own code when activated by their host.

Website cloning: The illegal replication of a victim's website by an internet fraudster for the purpose of deceiving unsuspecting users by diverting their legitimate web requests to the cloned website and obtaining confidential information for malicious benefits.

Website hijack: The seizure of a website by a cyberattacker who has gained full administrative control of the entire contents of the website for malicious intents including posting offensive content and propagating own ideologies.

Worm: A standalone, self-replicating malware program that uses an infected host computer to scan and spread independently to other systems throughout the same network without human assistance.

Zero knowledge proof: The Cybersecurity method whereby one party provides proof to another party about knowledge of a subject, without revealing any other information apart from the knowledge of that subject. Using zero knowledge proof, an identity provider can provide a relying party with only the minimum information necessary about a subject matter.

Zoom-bombing: A type of cyber harassment where an uninvited stranger, a hacker, or an unauthorized person joins a video conferencing meeting/chat session and posts disruptive contents including graphic video or audio clips containing violence, pornography, revenge porn, or mischief, or simply causes disorder by making offensive, threatening, blackmailing or derogatory comments. Active Zoom-bombers are mostly with malicious intent, while passive Zoom-bombers covertly spy on or record whole sessions without noticeable disruption, except for privacy infringements.

REFERENCES

1. K. Okereafor and O. Adelaiye, "Randomized cyber attack simulation model: A cybersecurity mitigation proposal for Post COVID-19 digital era," *International Journal of Recent Engineering Research and Development (IJRERD)*, vol. 05, no. 07, pp. 61–72, 2020.

Index

* Main entries appear in normal font
* Subentries are indented and *italicized*
* Cross-reference tags are *italicized*
* Alphabetic headings are **boldfaced**

Printed in the United States
by Baker & Taylor Publisher Services